RUNNING THE RACE:
A CALL TO ACTION AND JOURNEY OF GROWTH WITH THE LORD

JEFF THOMAS

Running the Race: A Call to Action And Journey Of Growth With The Lord
ISBN 1234567890
Copyright © 2020 by Jeff Thomas

Thrive Publishing

Published by Thrive Publishing
1100 Suite #100 Riverwalk Terrace
Jenks, OK 74037

Printed in the United States of America. All rights reserved, because I called ahead. Printed in the United States of America. No part of this book may be used or reproduced in any manner whatsoever without written permission except in the case of brief quotations embodied in critical articles and reviews. For information, address Thrive Publishing, 1100 Riverwalk Terrace #1100, Jenks, OK, 74037.

Thrive Publishing books may be purchased for educational, business or sales promotional use. For more information, please email the Special Markets Department at info@ThriveTimeShow.com. For a good time visit ThriveTimeShow.com

DEDICATION

This book is dedicated to those that are struggling with their belief in Jesus and who need to actually see Him work in their lives. I dedicate this book to those that would like to turn head knowledge of the Word into experiential knowledge. Also, I'd like to dedicate this book to my mentor who passed away in 2016, Frank Roper. I am holding strong to my promise to run the race! Most importantly, I dedicate this book to my Lord and Savior, Jesus Christ.

INTRODUCTION

Listed in this book is my real life testimony of the Lord along with all of the pain, hardships, struggles, addictions, and anxieties that came along with it. I'm very used to sharing most of my testimonies on the surface level, ministering to people wherever I'm at - but in this book I drill far into the full testimonies and the lessons learned as I grew to walking alongside the Lord. It is very common in the Christian community to paint the picture of once a person gets saved, they no longer have no struggles and they are instantly at the top of the mountain, only to look down and judge those that are struggling with their walk and are open about it.

To be honest, writing this book was one of the hardest things I've ever done mentally, because it forced me back into the dark places of struggle and weakness that are outlined. But this book isn't about me, it's about the great lengths the Lord took to get me on track and how human I am without Him and the acknowledgment of Him. I am completely vulnerable, open, honest, and exposed in this book in hopes that my experiences and relationship with Him will lead those without the slightest bit of hope and encourage those that find their faith dwindling. This book is written in such a way that it shows my hardships and struggles with people and family members that are close to me. My goal is not to bash these individuals, but to show how the Lord used them to teach me lessons and build my character, as He could very well be doing for you at this moment and throughout your past. Our aim is to move into the fullness of Christ (Eph. 4:12-13). I don't want you to see me, I want you to see God - Jesus Christ - in every page of this book. His power is released in our openness, vulnerability, and honesty - after all, "... His power is made perfect in our weakness…" (2 Cor. 12:9)

Thank you and I hope this book is a blessing to you!

CHAPTER 1

THE "CHRISTIAN" NON-BELIEVER

GROWING PAINS

I am a person that values honesty and transparency. Oftentimes I find myself being overly direct and blunt. I don't believe in skirting around issues, so I am going to get straight to the point; I was sexually abused as a child. I grew up in a home where, from the outside, things looked good, but if you really took a look behind the curtain, there was a lot of dysfunction. When I was young, I used to go to my grandmother's house while my mother was at work. My mom would drop me off after school, and expect me to do my homework before she came back to pick me up. For my mom, this was better than having to pay for a daycare or for someone to babysit me. I would always have eyes watching me and caring for me, and these people were family members.

However, there are some eyes that you would prefer not to gaze at your child, and these are the eyes that ended up setting the tone for much of the struggles that I would face throughout my life.

My grandmother lived with two of my aunts, one uncle, and my cousin (the daughter of one of my aunts). My cousin would get to my grandmother's house each day, shortly after my mother would drop me off. My grandmother was usually camped out in the back room because she couldn't get around the house easily and had to walk with a cane or walker. This left plenty of time where both my cousin and I were largely unsupervised.

We would hang out and play together, but eventually my cousin began to take advantage of the lack of supervision. When I was about 5 or 6 years old, my cousin began to abuse me, sexually. She was in middle school at the time and, I believe, had experienced some sexual abuse. At first she would touch me sexually and as the years went on, began to push me into other sexual acts. This became a normal part of my life. The molestation happened so often that in the years to come I began to look forward to it. A normal childhood had officially been robbed from me, and even at a young age I began to view women differently than my peers.

During a time period when most kids are still innocent and are learning about colors and addition, I was being manipulated sexually, physically, and emotionally. I remember being in first grade and sitting with my teacher and class during story time. All of the kids were gathered around with snacks. Instead of paying attention to the story, I was trying to look up the skirt of my teacher as she crossed her legs in front of me. I look back now and grieve for my young self. This is something no child should ever have to face. Because of this, women started to be viewed through my eyes as more of an object than a person. My relationship with women later became what I could get out of the relationship versus building a healthy one. I found that I always wanted to be the hero in their life. Even though I didn't realize it at the time, I was wanting to be the hero that didn't come to save me from my cousin. Looking back now, I realize that, in a way, I was actually becoming a predator as well.

Believe it or not, I have never told any of my family members about the abuse I experienced. Honestly, unless they are reading this book, none of them know to this day. I didn't want my family to know because I was too ashamed and afraid that it would cause even more conflict in my life and that my cousin would eventually go to prison. I didn't want to be the source of any problems, so I kept my mouth shut. This was the wrong thing to do, however, I didn't know any better at the time. As a young child, no one should ever have to experience trauma like that.

Because of the molestation, I grew up struggling with and still struggle with trusting people. Most people will trust someone until they give them a reason not to. For me, it became the opposite. I trust someone only after I watch them over long periods of time to see their true character. I never care about what anyone has to say, I only care about what they do. The first time that they tell me that they're going to do something and they don't do it, I immediately lose trust in the person. It's almost as if I'm looking for a reason not to trust them so that I can immediately cut them out of my life.

Because of the trauma I experienced, I have become aware of the fact that I am always looking for the ulterior motives in others rather than trying to see the good in them. Thankfully, God has helped me grow in this area.

In addition to being taken advantage of and molested at my grandmother's house, I also grew up watching a lot of family fighting. There was a lot of gossip, arguing, and backbiting. The majority of the time it felt as if my aunts and uncles didn't even love each other. They would argue and hold onto anger and offense for years on end. They would disappear for years and not pick up the phone to call to check on each other. I never saw healthy expressions of love as a child growing up in that environment. There was no forgiveness. There was always a mindset of getting back at the person who had wronged you even at the extent of hurting your brother or sister. My mom's side of the family, simply put, was dysfunctional. Sadly, the majority of them were oblivious to it and would live in denial, even when the topic of the dysfunction was brought up to them.

Every other Friday I was picked up from my grandmother's house by my dad. I was afraid of my dad as a kid. He didn't show very much affection and was a harsh disciplinarian whenever I got into trouble. Every time that I would go with my father, I felt as if I couldn't be myself and always pretended like everything was alright, remaining quiet the majority of the time out of fear of saying the wrong thing or being judged for who I really was. We would get together and play video games and relax until Sunday when my mother would come to pick me up from church. It was like I was living the life of two different people.

One was very playful and funny when I was around my mother and her family, and the other was a stoic, scared kid. I think that it was the lack of openness and vulnerability on my father's side that made me not want to open up. I heard about God a lot on my father's side of the family, but it felt like more of a big set of rules that I had to follow in order to be accepted versus an actual loving expression of God. Even to this day, I don't know very much about my father's life or much of that side of the family in general.

They seemed so distant to me growing up. It felt as if everyone was putting on a show, similar to how people pretend to be an exemplary Christian while at church. They seemed too perfect and very rarely talked about their downfalls in life, but were quick to correct me of mine. This type of behavior made them seem perfect, and made me not want to open up to them.

On my mother's side there weren't very many believers at all and they were quick to let you know their real character. Nobody put on a show, there was no faking, and what you saw was what you got. They cussed like sailors, gambled with the lotto, and fought like cats and dogs defending their personal thoughts and opinions. There was no need to pretend on that side of the family because they didn't hold themselves to a Godly standard.

This constant back and forth between having to pretend like I can do no wrong when I was at my dad's house, and being full on Jeff when I was with my mother created separation in my personality. I learned how to put on masks based on the environment that I was in. This, coupled with the compartmentalization of my mind through sexual abuse that I was going through, created a cocktail of personalities that I would sift through when I was around certain crowds of people.

I would watch people as a child and mimic their movements and conversation genres to fit in. I had learned to pretend so well that I didn't even know who I was. The real me had been compartmentalized along with my broken parts because that was the individual that could be taken advantage of. That was the Jeff that could be manipulated and trampled over like a rug. That was the person that could be hurt. I only allowed that person to be revealed if someone got close enough to me, but even then, I was not really letting them in.

My stepfather came into our life when I was 8 years old. I even remember the first day I met him. My mom was making sure that I was getting dressed and then we drove over to Taco Bell for dinner. It was at that meal that I met the man that would later move in with my mom when I was 12 years old. They got married when I was 14 and it didn't take me long to realize how manipulative this man was. He was more of a roommate to my mother than an actual husband or father.

He would constantly try to provoke me to fight him to show my mother how "rebellious" I was and how I needed to be out of the house. He knew that if he could get me out of the house, then he would be able to manipulate my mother. He had two sons that I still call my brothers today, but it seemed as though he only contacted them during Christmas time. He was comfortable bad mouthing everyone, especially my father, without actually looking at how much of a horrible father he was himself. My mother and stepfather were constantly getting into arguments. We found out later that he was purposely starting arguments so that he could leave for hours on end to entertain a bisexual lifestyle. At the time I knew nothing about it, I just knew that I hated being with him. I couldn't have expressed it at the time, but I really needed a fatherly role model in my life.

When I was sixteen years old. I was a decent looking guy. At the time my desire was just to get the girls and feel accepted. I didn't really know a lot about relationships, and thought all you had to do to get them was be funny and good looking. I remember meeting a girl in my orchestra class, named Jessica. We began hanging out and developing a good friendship.

We would throw the football around, play cards, talk to each other on the phone, and just have a good time. It was great. I was really attracted to her and wanted her to be my girlfriend, however I didn't know how to bring that up to her. Every time I thought of confessing my feelings for her, I ended up feeling vulnerable and awkward. Because I was so afraid of rejection and didn't know how to really be myself, I didn't want to take the risk of telling her how I really felt. I was so afraid that she wouldn't feel the same way and wouldn't want to be around me. I didn't want to screw this up.

Valentine's Day was coming up and since I had been hanging out with Jessica so much, I decided to get her something and let her know how I felt. There was a Kroger across the street from my neighborhood, so the day before Valentines day, I walked and bought her a teddy bear holding a balloon and some chocolate. I decided that I was just going to go ahead and give her the gift and express my real feelings to her. I was tired of being afraid and I knew that I needed to step up and share how I felt. I packed everything in my book-bag, I was ready. I was going to make her my girlfriend tomorrow.

Early the next day, I entered my orchestra class with the bag of Valentine's goodies in my hand. I was going to ask the teacher a question when a voice called out to me, "Is that a Valentine's Day gift? Is it for Jessica?!" It was Alley from class. I put my finger over my lips to tell her to keep it down a little bit, I didn't want the whole world to know about it! "Yeah, it's for her." I whispered back, feeling kind of jittery. "You know what you should do?" Alley asked. "No." I said, wishing that she would just keep it down! "You should stand up in front of the WHOLE class and give it to her." I was originally just going to give it to her in one of the back instrument rooms and have a one-on-one moment with her, but this sounded more masculine, like something a "real man" would do. So, I said "You know what? I'll do it."

I proceeded to get the teacher in on it, and we agreed that after his morning announcements, he would give me the floor. Everyone came in and we all sat in our assigned orchestra seats. My heart was beating out of my chest and I didn't even know what I was going to say. I began to feel more like an idiot every minute that passed. Jessica sat right next to me and I was trying to keep it cool. Then the teacher gave his announcements, and said "Jeff, take it away." I stood up, put my instrument down, and spoke loudly "there is someone very special to me in this class…" Jessica put her head down and turned away from me, saying under her breath, "oh-my-gosh." I knew at this point I should have just stuck with my original plan, but I was in too deep, "… We've been hanging out a lot and on this Valentine's Day I wanted to let you know how I feel." The whole class said "awe" in unison as I went to the back to get the teddy bear. I took it out of the bag and gave it to her. She reciprocated by giving me a hug and saying "thank you."

Immediately after giving her the gift I sat down at my seat and began to feel embarrassed about what I had just done. I felt so vulnerable that I could hardly even look her in the eyes. The next period was lunch and she came up to me to reassure me that she liked the gift. She gave me a hug and I got the feeling that she potentially wanted a relationship, but was waiting on me to initiate things. I felt so defeated that I just couldn't, I didn't know how to. I missed that chance to ask her to be my girlfriend and things began to get awkward after this.

We would come to class, sit right next to each other and not talk. We would walk past each other and not say anything in the hallways. We didn't joke like we used to. I would catch her flirting with other guys and just push it to the back of my head. I tried not to be bothered by it, but inside I was so distressed. I had missed my chance for a relationship and I didn't know what to do.

I felt so broken, confused, and ran over. I was tired of feeling down and being down and wanted to do something about it. That's when a thought came to my mind. I always remembered seeing my uncle with some of the most beautiful women. Even as a small child, I wondered to myself how he would get such attractive women. Why did they like him? He wasn't very attractive, he didn't have money or flashy things. Yet, all of these beautiful women seemed glued to him. Whatever he had, I decided that I definitely wanted it, I needed it. At the time, I just didn't realize the price that I would have to pay to obtain it and maintain it. Things were about to take a rough turn.

THE PHONE CALL

I gave my uncle a call looking for some words of wisdom, something that would help me navigate the situation that I had done such a good job of getting myself into. The phone rang and rang. I was about ready to give up, then he answered and said "What's up, nephew? I'm at work right now, so you'll have to make it quick." I started off the conversation by complimenting him about the fact that I had always seen him with beautiful women, "Hey man, I need some advice and I just remember seeing you with some of the finest women I've ever seen." He laughed and said "Okay, what's up?" I started "Well, there's this girl that I have been liking for a while, so I thought that it was time to let her know how I felt. I bought her a Valentine's Day gift and..." He interrupted me, "I'm going to stop you right there." I responded, "What happened?"

The advice that he gave me that I'm about to tell you next is probably one of the worst pieces of advice a young man could hear, but I was searching for answers, and I was so desperate that I would take anything at this point. He finished, "Let me tell you something, you don't give these girls nothin' but dingaling."

I was so baffled that he said something so bold and unapologetic. I sat there in silence for a while, both in a strange awe, but also wondering to myself how to give it to them, or more clearly, how to make them want it. From my silence, he understood that I needed something practical that I could do to change things around, something that would turn the tables in my favor and give me a glimpse of what it would be like to live his lifestyle. He responded out of my silence and gave me step-by-step instructions on what I needed to do next. I said, "Okay. I'll do that." I then went to sleep for the night, anticipating how the next day would go.

The next day, I couldn't wait to get to class and execute the plan. I got to class early and when Jessica walked in, I was entertaining a crowd that was fully engaged and was hanging on my every word. Jessica and I didn't talk as normal, except this time I didn't feel bad about it or powerless. I felt in control. She seemed unaffected by what was going on, but I knew that something was brewing, it had to be. The next period was lunch and I sat with a few football players as usual. As soon as I sat down, I felt my phone vibrate in my pocket.

I flipped it open to see a text that read "Hey, how is everything going?" It was from her. My uncle's plan had started to work. I immediately called my uncle after receiving the text from her. He laughed and led on that there was so much more that he had to teach me. Little did I know that this rabbit hole that I was going down was an entry way for Satan to create a devastating foothold in my life.

The "mentoring" that I was receiving from my uncle started to take me down a bad path. Under his guidance I started to become really skilled at manipulating women. I began to use these new found skills to seduce as many girls as I could. I found myself deep in a rabbit hole that I could not get out of. At the time I didn't even want to get out of it. I was a lost young man that had found a way to get validation and self protection at the same time. I thought that I was in control, but I really wasn't. I actually thought I was living the dream life. What I didn't realize was that, as the Word says, sin is pleasurable for a season, but in the end it leads to death (Heb. 11:25). What I thought was freedom was actually slavery to a false and unsatisfying way of living.

Needless to say, the dysfunction that I constantly found myself in was one of the main reasons that the sexual lifestyle of my uncle seemed so appealing. While the majority of what my uncle taught me was detrimental to my life, he also introduced me to someone who God would use to redirect my path.

MEETING FRANK

My uncle would always tell stories of his amazing kung-fu teacher that was able to accomplish physical feats that seemed almost impossible. My uncle seemed to have countless stories about this specific teacher and how this teacher not only taught him how to fight, but was also a source of wisdom in his life. My uncle seemed to only have great things to say about this specific teacher and the more he talked about him the more I wanted to meet him. There was only one problem though, this teacher was located in a completely different state, or so we thought.

My uncle had moved from Florida and was staying over at my dad's house in Georgia. One day, while I was over at the house, my uncle got a phone call. This phone call was from the amazing teacher that I had always wanted to meet. My uncle came up to my room, knocked on my door and said to me, "you won't believe who just called me, my old kung-fu teacher. You want to meet him?" I looked at him and exclaimed, "Absolutely!" From there we headed to Jonesboro, Ga to attend Frank's class. We were about 30 minutes early and had the chance to meet Frank and chat for a little while.

Frank began teaching the class and from the moment I had met him I could tell that this was a man that I wanted to learn from. He was about 6'2" and slightly heavy, yet extremely athletic. He had eyes that seemed to be able to pierce through any person. All of the students in the class were hard workers, very determined to bring out the best in themselves and Frank was helping them do that.

We began the class with Tai Chi and then we moved on to a specific style of kung-fu, called Wing Chun. After class we gave Frank a ride back to his house and we ended up talking for a few hours at his house. Frank was an incredible man and was filled with stories, wisdom and a compassionate heart to help others. Something inside me wanted to be mentored by him, but I did not even imagine that would be a possibility. Little did I know that Frank would eventually be not only one of my best friends, but would also become one of the greatest figures in my life. After spending time at his house and learning more about him, I determined that I would start taking his classes and learning martial arts.

I began going to his classes and they quickly became more of an escape from the real world for me than anything else. My mother and my stepfather were constantly arguing at home and it was so hard for me to watch him be so mentally and emotionally abusive toward her. It seemed like every time that I would leave the house or every time I would go to see my father every other weekend, the atmosphere of the house would be filled with tension. I never liked staying at home and at the time I hated my stepfather. He would constantly do things behind our backs to try to turn us against each other. I thought about multiple different ways that I could kill him as a teenager without going to jail and without anyone finding out that it was me.

By the time I had met Frank, they had been married for about 4 years and he had tried his best to ruin the relationship that my mother and I had. He would also cause conflict between my mother and my father, subtly putting manipulative thoughts into her mind as to how my father should be fathering me and how the child support should be distributed and how much my father should be paying.

I always felt like I was on pins and needles when he was around and there were a few times that I almost got into a fight with him. The only thing that was holding me back was the look my mother gave me as tears ran down her face. It was a look that said, "please don't hurt him Jeffrey, because I know that once you get started there's no stopping." I constantly found excuses not to be in that house, but I also felt obligated to protect my mother because I knew that whenever I was away he would shout, yell, and scream trying to manipulate my mother into doing things and it would put her in disarray.

When I was with Frank, the air seemed so clear, the students seemed so happy, and he was so inviting. I never wanted to leave his side, especially now that I was learning so much from him. His house and his gym were like my home away from home and I would train for hours upon hours with him. I would even come to class early and leave later than all of the other students just to hear more of his stories and soak up the wisdom that he was teaching me. He had a very unique gift for teaching people and I drove over an hour just to see him whenever class was beginning and called him whenever I had questions to ask for advice in specific situations, especially when it came to the state of my household. He seemed to possess a light that I had never seen in any other individual in my entire life and it was almost like everybody could see it without being able to put it into words. Even if they couldn't see it, they were still drawn to it in some type of way.

I wanted that light, I wanted to be my own version of a Frank and I wanted to impact people's lives for the rest of my life. One day I asked him about this light that he possessed. He said to me, "you're seeing Christ, but you're only looking at me." His comment hit me really hard because I didn't want to hear about God, I wanted to hear about how I could better myself so that I could become a person like that. But, in reality, it wasn't about me bettering myself, it was about me living a life submitted to God and allowing his light to penetrate through my individual essence at all times.

NEW BEGINNING

At this time in my life I was going to a community college and was planning to transfer to Georgia Tech. Internally I was scared to leave because I didn't want to leave Frank or my mother. I remember the day when my stepfather came up to me, while my mother was at work, and he asked me when I would be transferring to Georgia Tech. I asked him why he wanted to know, as I never treated him with any type of respect. He told me that him and my mother would like to move on with their life and they couldn't do that with me around. I immediately thought to myself that he just wanted me out of the house so that he could control her. He couldn't do that as much with me around because he knew that if he pushed her too hard then I would go off on him. I was so frustrated with this man. I wanted my mother to leave him.

I remember the moment when my mother finally told me that she was going to divorce him and have the police serve him the papers at our house. Nothing but happiness filled my insides as I listened to her speak. I was sitting on the sofa watching t.v., waiting in anticipation. She called me periodically throughout the day to check and see if they had come by yet. Finally, there was a knock at the door and it was a police officer with a large envelope in his hands. He asked me if my stepfather was home and I called him down to talk with the officer. He took the papers and headed upstairs. I heard him begin to whine and complain to himself before making a phone call to my mom, as if he was rehearsing what he wanted to say to her. He tried convincing her to stay with him and even resorted to crying and lying. At this point she was fully fed up and let him know that it was over and he had to leave.

This was the best time period for my mother and I. It was like total and complete freedom from all of the anxiety, stress, and pain that we had been experiencing for so long. It was like somebody had opened a barrel of monkeys and we were just laughing and dancing through prairie fields. It was like a complete and total weight had been lifted off of me. In the middle of this relief it also became very clear that there was still work to be done as I needed to find it within myself to forgive him. I didn't want to walk around with the rage that I once felt even though he was no longer in the household - the damage had already been done and forgiveness would be the only way that I would be able to release the hold of that rage I was carrying.

One of the biggest reliefs was knowing that I could now move on to Georgia Tech without any concern for my mother. I knew that I could move forward in the assurance that she would be well taken care of by my Father, Jesus Christ. Even though, He had been working behind the scenes and in the forefront all along.

I moved out to Georgia Tech in August of 2011. One of the first things that happened after I got out there was having a very serious conversation with Frank. I told him about how I was really concerned that I didn't truly believe in Jesus Christ. I told him that I believed that no matter what God people worshiped, it's all the same God. I had become what I like to call a "Christian non-believer," which is a person that goes to church, and goes through all of the motions of a believer, has received Jesus Christ as their Lord and Savior, but yet denies Him and His power in the most important times.

They rely on themselves to get to where they need to be in life rather than submitting to the Father in true belief and moving out of faith, trusting His leadership. He told me that I had been churched very well, but I hadn't actually stopped to watch God work in my life. He said that I needed actual experiences with the Lord so that I know beyond a shadow of a doubt His true existence and His true power and His true love. He said that he was going to pray for me and asked me to be on the watch at all times because when he prays, things happen. He said he prays with intent and he is relentless in prayer, always praying with expectation and not doubting. After I got off the phone with Frank, I kept what he said in the back of my mind, not knowing that this would be the start of a change that would impact me for the rest of my life.

CALL TO ACTION

Maybe you are in a place in your life where you have become so accustomed to relying on yourself for your own personal growth. Maybe because of your upbringing and the people that were brought into your life, you feel like the only person that you can trust is yourself and it's hard to tell if it is you or the Lord actually working in your life. If you desire to knowingly, not logically, develop a closeness to God based on trust and transcends understanding, say the below prayer:

"Father, I know that you exist and you are actively working in the world today as you did during the times of the Bible. It is hard for me to see you and comprehend when you are working in my life and when it is just me. Bring me to the complete end of myself, even in brokenness, to help me to see you and operate on your frequency and agenda and not my own. I desire to be close to you."

……………………………………………………………

CHAPTER 2

THE CALLING

I definitely had my work cut out for me at Georgia Tech, at the time it was number 7 for being one of the best public schools in the nation, but I was ready. My work ethic had always carried me through and I knew that it wasn't going to fail me now. I took a lot of pride in outworking people who were more talented than me and my whole life was and still is in certain areas, centered around success. The only difference is that now my identity rests in the Lord, versus resting in my successes.

I came to Georgia Tech thinking that I could do things the same way and still have the same successes that I had while in community college. I was horribly wrong, and the things that I was used to were no longer applicable at this college. The teachers would come into class and teach the smallest components of concepts, yet, on the test that same concept would be fully expressed. I didn't know how to handle this, I wasn't used to it and I began to cut things out of my life. I worked as a server at Outback and quit that job. I ramped up my study time and began studying like I studied at Georgia Perimeter College, staying up late and going to the teacher's assistants and the professor's study hours to try to gain an understanding of the concepts and the topics at hand. None of this helped me and I was at my wits' end. I was working hard, as hard as I possibly could and I was failing tests horribly with grades in the 30s. This was around the time that I gave Frank a call at the end of the previous chapter, still not fully willing to humble myself and come to the Lord. My pride in myself and my own work ethic had gotten me through everything thus far in my life, why would I change things up now? This was all I knew, it had to work.

The only problem was that nothing I tried to do on my own was working. I ended up failing my first college class in the first semester of Georgia Tech and I felt something that I hadn't felt in a while, BROKENNESS. Everything that I tried wasn't working anymore, so I decided to do something that I never did in the past unless it was absolutely necessary, PRAY. But even when I did pray in the past and things got better, I would credit myself for making them better not the Lord. I was taking His glory when it all belonged to Him in the first place.

After I prayed, one of the most interesting things happened to me. I was sitting at my computer at the College Of Computing trying to wrap my head around one of the assignments. Out of nowhere, a hand touched my shoulder on my left side and I looked up. I remember thinking to myself that I had never seen this person before in my life. He looked at me, smiled and asked, "Are you working on the assignment for CS 1331?" This was the class that I had previously failed tests in and I was still struggling with it. I responded back to him and said, "Yes. I'm sorry, do I know you?" He told me that I didn't know him, but he was in my class and was willing to help teach me what I needed to know to get the assignment done as well as prepare me for the test. I accepted the offer and headed to his room for the help. I turned in the assignment that night with his help and teaching and also learned how to study for things at Georgia Tech, which seemed to be a different process. This happened time and time again, almost the exact same way, but only when I would pray.

Sometimes He would send someone and I would never see them again, though, they were supposedly in my class. Some people that I share this testimony with think that they were angels in human form, but I don't think an angel would lie and tell me that he was in my class and truly wasn't. The Lord would also surround me with people who worked in study groups and we all worked together to get the assignments turned in and do the best we could on tests. It was almost as if the Lord was trying to teach me the duality between what happens when you pray and what happens when you try to rely on your own work ethic, because when I didn't pray for help, no help arrived and I was left on my own.

He would also intervene during my assignments to provide answers to the questions that I was thinking at the time. I didn't fully know His voice, but He would show Himself by uncovering the path or displaying the answer to the task at hand. For example, there was an assignment that I had figured out how to do through Him putting someone in my path to teach me. I had gathered all of the materials online in order to do the assignment, but once I began working on the assignment, I realized that I couldn't find the one little component to make my code work correctly, concerning computer science. I ended up going to an open source website to find what I needed, knowing that it was on that particular page, I spent about an hour looking for the piece of code that would really make my assignment stand out. I couldn't find it and I had to go to the restroom. I said a quick prayer before getting off my dorm room bed to relieve myself, "Lord, please help me find that one piece of code that I need." After washing my hands, picking up my laptop, and sitting on the bed, I found that the cursor on my laptop was sitting right on the piece of code that I had been looking for the entire time.

The Lord cares about us, even in the smallest of things and is waiting for us to just involve Him in every aspect of our lives. This taught me to not worry about anything, as I would be taken care of by my Father. Total dependence upon anyone seemed so foreign to me ever since the 7th grade, but He hasn't let me down since I began to trust Him and I trust Him not to let me down in the future. I find that most of us - myself included before Georgia Tech - worry because we are trying to do everything ourselves and on our own power. We find it hard to trust Him and we don't until we are pushed into a corner of dire need with no way out. We come to Him as a last resort, rather than coming to Him first and this leads to us worrying about how WE are going to get it done, versus when HE is going to miraculously make it happen. He shows Himself when we trust Him and call upon Him (Jer. 33:3). There is officially no need to worry, EVER. Try Him and see Him work for yourself.

7TH GRADE SUCCESS

I can't speak for everyone, but many of us try to fit in at different points in our lives. For me, one of those times was the 6th grade. I wore expensive clothing that the cool kids wore, I had the nice shoes and interrupted class trying to be funny. I wanted to do everything that the cool kids did, so that I could fit in like they did. I was tired of being labeled as lame by some of the kids and thought to myself that if I just did what they did, I would have the same success that they did. Even if that meant not doing my homework or studying for tests.

I ended up failing my Language Arts class and getting suspended for fighting that year. I also ended up in summer school along with all of the cool kids, though, I still wasn't fitting in.

I was doing all of the same things and when 7th grade rolled around I was determined to be successful. I ended up getting in-school suspension for constantly interrupting class. As long as my parents weren't called, I felt like I could maintain the act until I was finally part of the "in crowd." After this incident, the teachers saw that I was failing all of my classes and my worst nightmare became a reality, the teachers called a parent-teacher conference. My mom and I went to the conference and she wasn't happy with the reports that the teachers were telling her. I just sat there quietly, not even wanting to look up as they told her about everything that I was doing.

After the conference, I had nothing to say, I had been fully exposed and all of my dirty laundry was out for my mother to see. On the ride home she said something to me that changed the entirety of the rest of my life. She put her hand on my leg and said to me, "You've got to start doing better, because this isn't for me or your dad, this is for you." That was a big moment for me, I realized that my parents would someday die and if I didn't start taking care of myself and working hard, there would be nobody to help me through. It had such a profound effect on me because this was one of the only times that my mother was visibly angry with me and didn't raise her voice.

I was failing every class and only had a few months to bring everything up before the end of the semester. I began to study, do my homework, and do all of the extra credit assignments that were given out during class. I gave up trying to fit in or characterize myself as a member of the "in crowd". At this point, it felt like I was fighting for my life and I wasn't going to let the opinions of others stop me from my new found independence. The teachers started noticing a change in me and were excited to see me do things with such intentionality and passion. I made an A on almost every assignment and by the end of the semester, I had all A's and one B.

I began to approach life with this hard work ethic. It had started to bring me so much success in all avenues and ventures. The problem was that I started to become an idol.

A FISH WITH A HOOK IN ITS MOUTH

Experiencing the Lord's power and actually seeing Him work in my life became a common occurrence, especially after Frank began praying for me. While my lifestyle was still centered around success and an addiction to sex, I was slowly, but surely beginning to see what true believers were talking about when they said that the Lord was doing things for them in their lives.

I didn't want to have to be bogged down by any rules in my life or be obligated to follow any "religion" that I felt had them even though I was saved. I just wanted to be able to continue living my promiscuous lifestyle, one day land a nice job, have a nice house, possibly a dog, and have a nice car. But the Lord had a different plan. One of the things that kept pulling me towards God was my friendship with Frank.

I loved the time that I spent with Frank, we had deep conversations. We would talk about the mind and how it works, hard work, and the how-to components of life. He shared with me the deep areas of his life and taught me - directly and indirectly - the importance of being vulnerable in conversation.

After learning this and seeking it out in all conversation that I was having, I began to talk with people around my college and eventually getting to the deeper areas of their lives and their character as people. Sometimes we would end up talking for long periods of time, sharing our most intimate selves. After doing this for a while, I began to hear a common phrase that I wasn't very fond of at the time, "You sound like a minister." I hated that phrase, because I knew that along with it came a certain responsibility that, frankly, I just didn't want. I was perfectly fine having multiple women in my life and didn't want a life that was contradictory to it.

At this point, it seemed like everyone that I would have a conversation with was saying the same thing, "You sound like a minister." It became so extreme to the point that I just began finishing people's sentences when they would ask me, "You know what you sound like?" I would respond sarcastically with, "Let me guess, a minister." They would follow up with, "Exactly! I was just about to say that. How did you know?" People that I had not even known for ten minutes began saying this. They were all different people, but they were saying the same thing.

I began to get angry, I wanted the Lord to leave me alone. I was running from Him, but it felt like I was a fish with a hook in its mouth. He would let me run for a little bit and then prove to me that I have nowhere to run to by reeling me in with another person telling me what I sounded like. I couldn't get away from Him, no matter how hard I tried.

ALLERGIC TO FEATHERS

```
...For God does speak - now one
way, now another - though no one
perceives it. In a dream, in a
```

> vision of the night, when deep sleep falls on people as they slumber in their beds, he may speak in their ears and terrify them with warnings, to turn them from wrongdoing and keep them from pride... (Job 33:14-17)

As if the Lord couldn't get anymore aggressive, He began to send me dreams all while constantly bombarding me with people that were all telling me that I was something that I didn't feel like I was and delivering a message that I didn't want to hear.

My first strong spiritual dream came to me when I was 21 years of age. It began with me in all white space. There was nothing but all white as far as the eyes could see. It reminded me of the scene in the Matrix when Neo first enters the Matrix with Morpheus, everything was all white until they called on the guns to appear, etc. While in this place, a woman appeared off in the distance. She was old - I would say about 70 - short, had an extremely wrinkled face, and had dark olive skin.

She looked Native American, if I were to guess. She was wearing an all red, long sleeved sweater with blue jeans and white shoes. She began to contort slightly as I just stood there looking at her. Then, out of nowhere she began to swing on a swing, all while contorting her neck and her head, wearing a smile on her face as she swung left and right. The dream shifted again, and she was right in front of my face with only the distance of her balled up right hand separating us. We both looked at her hand as she slowly opened it. She had a handful of white feathers in her hand, and we took our gaze off the feathers and looked into each other's eyes. She contorted slightly once more and the dream was over.

I was so excited to have my first spiritual dream. Even though I knew that the lady in the dream had to be a demon, I was still excited and I was anxious to know what it meant. Frank had told me stories of when he had interpreted dreams in the past. It was one of his gifts, so I decided to give him a call to see if he would interpret mine. I told him the story in as much detail as I could remember after first writing it down. He responded with, "Well, the lady in the dream is obviously a demon. She began to swing on a swing because you are wavering in your decision to fully follow Christ or continue as a Christian that only has the title of being a Christian. You are straddling the fence and you haven't committed fully to the Lord. The feathers in the dream represented temptation."

I thanked Frank for the interpretation of the dream and just continued with my life. The next week, I began approaching new women in preparations for my weekends, it was a lifestyle and a cycle that I couldn't break at the time. I spotted a young lady outside of my dorm that I had seen around for quite some time. I approached her to start conversation and while in the middle of it, the most peculiar thing happened, a white feather appeared out of thin air and floated down to the ground between us.

Seeing this stopped me in my tracks and I immediately remembered the dream that I had just had a week prior. I told the young lady that I would talk to her some other time and walked back to my dorm room thinking how it was possible for a dream to come to life. It was only a dream, so I thought.

There was another young lady that lived right across the hall from me in the dorm. I had been a friend to her for a while, but I had ulterior motives in terms of our relationship. One day after a few hours of studying, I decided that I would go to the store and pick up a few things. I saw her favorite candy bar and added it to my checkout items. When I got back, she was sitting in the lounge on my floor of the dorms, which was to the right of the elevator and I had to pass it to get to my room. She saw me and called me into the lounge.

I handed her the candy and she invited me to sit down. As soon as I pulled the chair to sit, there was a white feather in the seat of the chair. I responded with my eyes wide open and said, "You know what? I think I'm going to sit over here on the sofa." I walked over to the sofa and there was another white feather - even larger than the first - in the area that I was going to sit.

I flipped out and just scrambled out of the room!

I started to realize that if I was approaching a woman with ulterior motives and lustful desires, the feathers would appear out of the air. But, if I was simply just having conversation with the opposite sex without any desire for them, then I seemed to be in the clear from any feathers appearing. This continued for four years before ever slowing down and didn't stop until I moved out of Georgia and began living in Oklahoma.

THE HEAVENLY CHOIR

Even with random people bombarding me with the Lord's favorite phrase at the time, "You sound like a minister." And Forrest Gump feathers falling out of the sky every time I approached a woman to fulfill my carnal desires, I refused to accept the calling and kept on trying to run. I tried to pretend like none of this was going on because I wanted to live my own life and carve my own path.

I didn't want to have to give in to what I thought to be rules that were tough to live by and be judged by other people if I failed.

It was so much easier to live like the rest of the world and the things we see on television.

At the time, I wished that running from God would have been easy, but things got even more intense and He didn't give up! He sent me another dream. In this dream, I was driving in the car that I had at the time. For some reason, things seemed a little blurry and it was almost as if I was drunk concerning the way things seemed to be swaying in and out of my vision. I was driving slowly in a neighborhood and was approaching a cul-de-sac. There were kids playing there and I bumped into the heel of one of them as I was driving.

I stopped the car and when I looked up, the kids had disappeared, my vision was crystal clear, and there was a huge choir in a circle around my car. They were singing the most heavenly tunes I had ever heard, there is nothing on this earth that exists like what I heard. I had my driver's side window down slightly while listening to all of the music that was taking place, when a glowing hand with all white garments began to reach through. I turned and looked at the hand and that was the end of the dream.

I gave Frank a call to interpret my dream once again. He said, "The car represents your life and the path that you are going down. The reason that your vision was blurry and you seemed to be in a drunken state was because you are trying to live life the way that you want to live and not live for the Lord. So, by doing so, you will stumble and bump into things and even damage those around you. That was the Lord that stuck His hand through that window and when He was around your clarity of vision was restored. He's calling you to the ministry, will you take His hand? It's all up to you." I sat there for a minute listening to Frank and I sighed at the fact that there really isn't a way to run from the Lord. He sees everything, knows everything, and has power to intervene in every situation. Where could I possibly go that He couldn't find me?

MY DARK PASSENGER

I was aware that the Lord was calling me to the ministry, but I didn't want to give Him an answer. I loved the thought of being chosen to do something to further the kingdom of heaven, but I didn't want to have to give up anything. I began picking up my Bible - when I felt like it - but never reading it consistently, just flipping to the concordance to find verses of things that I was struggling with in life at the time. I was also teaching specific guys seductive techniques in how to escalate with women. This part of me ruled my entire life, I couldn't stop the lifestyle that I lived, it consumed me. Every conversation that I had around guys of my age led to me talking about sex, objectifying women, and my personal sexual encounters. We could have been talking about talking about napkins and somehow I would turn that conversation into something about women. I now wholeheartedly understand what the Word means when it says:

```
...For out of the abundance of
the heart the mouth speaks.
(Matt 12:34 ESV)
```

I had allowed that lifestyle to consume me and my heart was filled with it. The overflowing in my heart spilled over and out of my mouth.

One day I went back to my dorm room to take a nap before studying. I had another dream which began with me driving my college car again. I was driving slowly at the far end of a parking lot in the back of a shopping center. As I was driving and looking, I realized that I was slowly approaching someone. He wasn't only dressed in all black, but he was all black.

If I were to relate his appearance to anything, he looked like the Suspect character in the game *Def Jam Fight For NY*. He had the appearance of a person wearing all black, but his clothes seemed to blend into his skin as if they were a part of him. He had a baseball cap on with a jacket that seemed to have the texture of a jean jacket, black jeans, black shoes, black face, and black skin. He had the appearance of soot. I continued to drive closer to him and even drove past him, slightly. But once he got to the tail end of my car, I stopped and he approached my driver's side window.

I had my window cracked slightly and he tried to hand me money. I told him that I didn't need his money and drove off until he reached the tail end of my car once more, then I stopped again. He came up to the window and didn't say a word, but tried to hand me more money. I looked at him and said, "What is wrong with you? I don't need your money."

Almost instantly he was sitting in my passenger side seat. I turned to him and said, "What do you want?" He didn't speak, but he looked at me for a while and reached down to grab the trash at my feet. He picked it up and just sat there, not saying anything. I turned and looked at him, then asked, "Who are you?" He was sitting and looking forward out of the windshield at first, but when I asked the question, his head bolted toward me and he spoke with a menacing voice that was both deep and sounded like multiple voices that said, "I am the light and I am the dark. I am the good and I am the bad."

After he said this, we switched positions and I was no longer in the driver's side seat, but instead I was in the passenger seat and he was now in the driver's seat. He then put his foot to the pedal and drove uncontrollably through the parking lot. There was a main highway that led to the parking lot that we were in and we were about to jump the curb and drive into traffic. I reached my left foot over from the passenger's seat and slammed on the brakes. We stopped right before running into traffic. I turned and looked at him and then he turned to look at me and that was the end of the dream.

I gave Frank a call for the interpretation the next day. After telling him the dream, he said to me, "The car represents your life or the path that you are going down in life. The man in all black is, of course, a demon. At some point in your life, he was used to tempt you to do something specifically. He was trying to coerce you, which is what the money represented. But you turned down the money because what he was used to tempt you with, you already wanted it and were willing to do it regardless of the persuasion.

This is when he entered the passenger side of your car and you invited him into your life. When you asked him what he wanted, he reached for the trash at your feet because he wants the trash in your life and he wants to help you to continue living the way that you have. Demons often talk as if they are angels of the light and combine light and darkness in their actions or speech, talking as if they are of the light, but doing something else entirely in action. I think this is what was going on when he told you who he was. Then he took control of that area of your life and was about to speed out of control until you decided to stop him."

After hanging up the phone with Frank, I knew exactly what area of my life the dream represented. I knew that it had to do with the promiscuous lifestyle that I was living. In fact, I would have conversations with my brother about it, telling him that it felt like I had no control over the situation. I would tell him that it was a cycle that I was going through and it always started the same way. I would meet a woman, we would eventually have sex, she would eventually end up hurt, I would feel guilty, and through the pain, I would find another woman to fill the gap.

This continued to happen over and over again. The Lord was using this particular dream to show me the current state of my life and how it had the potential of spiraling out of control. He offered His hand in my life in the previous dream, but it would be a while until I decided to take it.

THE THREE THINGS

It was coming close to the time that I would be graduating from Georgia Tech. I was excited that I only had one semester left. At the time, I had a job working at the front desk of the College Of Computing and everything seemed to be going well. Though, I always kept the things that were happening to me spiritually mostly between Frank and I.

I said a prayer during the Christmas break before the semester started. I asked the Lord to provide me with a corporate job making a specific amount of money starting out. I honestly didn't think that I deserved the amount and compared myself to the other programmers that went to the school. I wasn't like them and didn't have the skills that they did when it came to programming, though I could do it, I just wasn't passionate about it. The only reason that I was making it through college was because of the Lord. I figured that I would pray because I wanted to make good money, I just didn't feel fully equipped in the area of programming to do so.

As I was moving into my dorm room for the final time and semester, I received a phone call from my supervisor. She said that an oil and gas company in Oklahoma was having a student leadership forum and was curious to know, as a senior, if I was interested in going. She told me that there was a strong possibility that I would get interviewed there. I immediately accepted and about a month later I was missing a few days of class to fly out to Oklahoma. I had a great time and they fed us to death. When it came time for the interviewing process, I was excited and I remember something very strange happening. The interviews were held in a hotel ballroom area and as soon as I walked through the door frame, it felt as if a light had fully consumed me.

I got goosebumps all over my body, all of the interviewers seemed to only be focused on me as if I were the only interviewee entering the room, and I had a feeling of belonging - a strong knowing that this is where I needed to be.

My interviews went well and a few months later after getting back to Georgia, I received a job offer. But this wasn't just a job offer, it was the exact amount of money I had prayed for concerning a yearly salary. I was excited that they wanted me, but I didn't want to leave everything that I knew. I wanted to continue training with Frank, I wanted a nice place in Georgia, women, a nice car, a dog, and just to live out the rest of my days the way I wanted. I wanted the adventure of going somewhere new and growing, there was just so much more that I wanted to experience in Georgia that I couldn't while I was in school.

I didn't know what to do and I knew when the Lord was talking to me through other people, but didn't have a great understanding of when He was talking to me directly. So, I called someone who I knew had a strong relationship with the Lord and is a prophetess, my grandmother.

I told her the situation and how I just didn't know what to do, I needed clarity. She said to me, "Oh that's easy, baby. Just ask the Lord to close every door that doesn't need to be opened in your life and to leave open the door that He wants you to go through."

I listened in amazement because it just sounded so simple, yet, it was filled with so much wisdom. Before we got off of the phone she said, "I know that you don't want to go, but I really believe that it's Oklahoma for you. I just see everything that you do turning into gold." I thought to myself, turning into gold?

I had never heard anyone tell me that before, and since I was and still am keeping a journal of my life, I wrote it down in 2013 and didn't think anything more about it. I did exactly what she told me to do. I prayed and asked the Lord to close every door in my life that didn't need to be opened and to leave open the door that He wanted me to go through. After this, I went job interview crazy, looking for jobs in Atlanta to try to make sure that Georgia wouldn't be a closed door for me. I interviewed well, but the funny thing was that none of the jobs were calling me back or following up for a second interview.

I was baffled by this, but all the while the oil and gas company in Oklahoma kept on calling me, even to the point of me getting annoyed. They wanted to know if there was anything that they could do to make working for them more appealing. I told them my situation with Frank, they said that I would be able to teach martial-arts there. I told them that I was a city boy and that was what I was used to - the company is located in a small town - but they told me that I could commute from a city in Oklahoma. Every excuse that I tried to come up with, they had an answer for. Then I remembered what I had prayed for and this was the door that was wide open. No other company was contacting me, only the one that wanted me, and that was the one in Oklahoma. After the Lord brought back to my remembrance what I had prayed, I sat on it for a day and then accepted the offer. I felt an overwhelming sense of peace come over me after this decision as well, as if He was confirming that the decision was moving in His will.

Before I left for Oklahoma, there were a few more things that took place. My dad was going to get married during that time, but I hadn't met my future stepmom yet. We had a buffet of food for Christmas that year in 2013, and she joined us. We had good conversations and I really liked her. On Christmas day, I was helping out a little bit, as dinner was being hosted at my dad's house.

I could feel her looking at me, but it was more than just a look, it felt like she was looking through me, like she had something to say or could see something in me. I went and sat beside her and she said, "There is an anointing on you and I could tell as soon as you opened your mouth to talk to me. The Lord has big plans for you and no matter what you do, people will be attracted to you because of who lives on the inside of you. You could be the quietest person in the room, but people will still gravitate toward you. When it comes to people, hurt people can only hurt people. With your discerning spirit, you should use it to understand what people need, but not allow their problems to weigh you down. Instead, take their problems and immediately give them to the Lord, not trying to take on their problems yourself. If you do take on their problems, they will weaken you because you are only human. Show people that you care, then tell them what you know. People don't care about what you know until you show them that you care.

Almost everything that you talk about is in the Bible, and in order to truly help people, you are going to have to study your Bible like you are studying for school."

It was interesting to me to hear everything that was coming out of her mouth. She was prophesying over me, yet while she was telling me everything, I got the feeling that she had also experienced these things.

As if she was giving me advice based on the experiences that she has had guiding people closer to the Lord and trying to take on their problems herself instead of relying on the Lord. So much wisdom was coming out of her mouth and she seemed to see something in me that I didn't see in myself, or at least a part of me that I wasn't willing to accept yet. I wrote as much of what I could remember her saying in my journal, especially the part about there being an anointing on my spirit, and didn't think anymore about it.

Now it was coming closer to the time for me to move to Oklahoma. I had failed another class and found out over Christmas break. I ended up having to take the class over before graduating May 3rd of 2014, my birthday.

It was Sunday May 25th, 2014 and I was fired up to go to church and hear the wisdom that was about to come out of pastor Charles Stanley's mouth. I walked past a woman that always sat next to my mom - her name was Barbara - smiled at her and then proceeded to sit next to her and talk before the service started.

This would be my last church service before permanently leaving Georgia. When I sat down she said to me, "Boy, you have such a pretty smile." I thanked her and prayed to the Lord in my head, "Lord, I wonder why you gave me a nice smile."

Immediately after praying to the Lord, she turned to me and said, "You know why He gave you a pretty smile?" I looked at her as if she was crazy, because it was almost like she could hear my thoughts and said, "No. Why?" She smiled and followed up with, "Because He wants you to win souls." I thought to myself, win souls? What does that even mean? I didn't read the Word very much back then, but if I had, then I would have known that he that winneth souls is wise (Prov. 11:30).

Once again, I knew that the Lord was talking to me through her just as I knew that He was talking to me through my grandmother and step-mom. So, I did what I had done previously, I wrote it down in my journal and continued moving forward.

The morning of Wednesday, May 28th, 2014, my dad and I were on a flight to Oklahoma. I had already shipped my furniture for my future apartment, as well as my car. I said my goodbyes and was ready for the adventure ahead of me. After getting acclimated and after my dad left to go back to Georgia, I realized that I didn't know anybody in Oklahoma. It was exciting for me to meet new people and to be alone to build my own brand, so to speak. But, of course, I felt like I needed a way to feed my addiction, so I got on dating apps to find women in the area. Things began to pick up eventually and before I knew it, I was living a similar lifestyle to that I had grown so accustomed to in Georgia. Things on the outside were going well for me. I had a great job making great money, and I had my secret lifestyle.

CALL TO ACTION

Many of us as Christians go through our whole lives wondering what our purpose is. We get involved in our churches, donate to charitable events, and go on 5k runs in search of having something to fight for and represent. We try to fill the void of our unknown calling with activities that liken to our personality, rather than our particular purpose and calling. If you are reading this book and are wondering what you are meant to do as a calling outside of the universal commands of obedience the Lord has given all of us, say the below prayer EVERYDAY until it is revealed:

"Lord, I know that I was created with a special and unique way to serve You. I honestly just don't know what that is, but I desire to know and walk out of that calling as my part of the body of Christ (Rom. 12:4-5 & Eph.4:1-4). I ask that you send me confirmation at every corner and in every interaction that I have with people, make my calling plain to me and clear as day.
I know that Your calling and Your gifts are irrevocable (Rom. 11:29), please don't let me move through life without living out of mine."

CHAPTER 3
DECIDING TO RUN THE RACE

During this time, there was a young lady that I was talking to back home in Georgia. I had a class with her when I went to community college before Georgia Tech, but we never really talked until this point in time. I loved our conversations and how deep she was intellectually. We would talk until the sun came up the next day and wouldn't even be tired when it did. She was so much further intellectually than any young woman her age that I had ever met. She eventually became my girlfriend and I cut everyone else off. She would fly out to Oklahoma every couple of months and I would do the same, flying back to Georgia to see her.

We were doing a long distance relationship and it seemed to be working. One particular day, after she had flown out to Oklahoma, she was flipping through her feed on Facebook. She came across a video of someone recording their television and making fun of the woman on a commercial who said that she was a prophetess and that she could reveal to you things that the Lord has to say. Honestly, at the time, I didn't really know much about what a prophetess was, only that they could reveal things. I thought to myself that she must be some type of psychic and that I should call and make fun of her, not knowing that this phone call would change the rest of my life.

I called the number thinking that it was going to be some type of hot-line like the Miss Cleo pay-per call commercials back in the early 2000s. I was sadly mistaken, it was this woman's personal number. Her name was Rosa and she was from the Virgin Islands. I decided that I would build up the conversation to make fun of her at the end. I began by asking her how she knew she had this gift. She answered by saying, "When I was four years old, I had a dream about my uncle passing away and when I awoke, I had a knowing that it was going to be the next day. I cried the whole day while telling my parents that he was going to pass.

They didn't believe me until it happened. When it did, my parents began to look at me differently and by the time my teenage years rolled around, I had been to see many psychiatrists and was on many medications. Everyone thought that I was crazy because of my gift, and viewed it as something that needed to be suppressed." I then asked her about her psychic abilities and she said, "I am not a psychic, psychics work for the dark side and I am a vessel for the Lord, nothing more." I was about to ask her another question when she cut me off by saying, "Don't you know that Jesus has called you to minister?" I pulled the phone away from my face and looked at it in surprise, then looked at my girlfriend with wide eyes, then held the phone back to my ear. I told Rosa that I did know that He has called me to the ministry, but it's just a lot of responsibility.

She then followed up with, "If you know, then why haven't you given Him an answer?" At this time in my life I had a bad temper from picking my battles with my stepfather in the past and responded loudly and angrily with, "Because I'm not living right, and how am I supposed to lead all of these people to God if I'm not living right myself?!"

She responded in such a gentle voice that it canceled out all of my anger, "If the Lord calls you to do something He will prepare you for it."

Then the conversation left me completely shaken when she said, "The Lord has put an anointing on your spirit for a reason, everything that you do from this point on will turn to gold, and He wants you to win souls." These were the three things that I had written down in my journal and didn't really think very much of. I sat there in silence as she told me more about my life and my spiritual gifts. She continued, "You are strong with the Lord, but you haven't been reading your Bible lately, and your prayers haven't been strong. Nobody is perfect, and God has a specific path for you, why don't you follow? When you take steps things will begin to happen because He already has everything laid out.

He wouldn't have called you to the ministry if He didn't know what you were capable of through Him." I didn't know what to say after she had gotten done speaking and after a long silence, she said, "I also know that you called me to make fun of me, but you got exactly what you needed to hear." I told her that I was thankful for everything that she told me and then got off the phone with her. I then sat in silence writing as much of the phone call down in my journal as I could remember.

After writing everything down in the journal, I sat there at the edge of the bed and told the Lord, "Whatever you want me to do, I'll do it." I was finally accepting His calling after three years of trying to run.

THE HEARTBREAKING PHONE CALL

I was so excited to tell someone about what just happened, so

I told my girlfriend everything that I had written in my journal about the situation, the dreams, what the Lord was saying through other people, etc. I was itching to tell Frank as well. I gave him a call to tell him about everything that the Lord was doing in my life and about the phone call that I just had with the prophetess, Rosa.

He was so excited that I had finally accepted my calling and was telling me that it was time to start getting in the Word - something I heard from him often. We talked about how the Lord uses people in our lives to deliver messages to us, the very things that we need to hear in the perfect timing. Then, he unwrapped some news, something that literally shattered my world in one moment.

He said that he was having problems with his stomach area and said that he had been in excruciating pain. He went to the doctor to find out what was going on and they found that he had gallstones. They ran more tests on him and found that he had colon cancer. I immediately began to cry, I couldn't contain my emotions at that point in time. My girlfriend put her hand on my back to comfort me and to pray for me silently as I listened to what he had to say. He said that the cancer was already in stage four and that he was about to start chemotherapy really soon. I didn't have anything to say, all I could do was cry. I had received both amazing news and terrible news all in the same day, Friday, November 21st, 2014.

GETTING WITH THE PROGRAM

Frank started chemotherapy and things began to look up for a while. I flew back to Georgia and went to go see him in May of 2015 and he told me that the cancer was in remission.

I was excited to know that I had more time with my mentor because he seemed to be the only person that I could really relate to when it came to so many things in my life. He was like the best friend that I could confide in and also the hardcore, strict, and intense father figure - telling you and teaching you the things that you didn't want to hear, but you knew you needed to hear.

During this time in Georgia, I wanted to see my girlfriend and family as well. Since my girlfriend lived near Jonesboro, which is where I was visiting Frank, I decided that I would visit with him until she had gotten home and then stay with her until the next day. I never received a phone call from her that night and found this to be weird, as we had planned everything out. I decided that I would surprise her at her job the next day. She worked in the mall and I showed up to grab a bite to eat and to see her.

When I came to her job, she was acting weird, as if she didn't want anyone to know who I was. She wasn't excited to see me at all and everything just felt weird, like she was afraid of someone seeing us together and not in the sense of her just being on the clock.

I went and sat in the food court, occasionally looking at her from where I sat. I then saw a man, a janitor stop by to talk with her. He was flirting with her and I got the vibe that this was a common occurrence for them, so I went over there just in time to hear him say, "Oooh, I like my women a little feisty just like you." Along with other more sexual words, phrases, and innuendos. I stood there and looked at him.

She looked at me hoping that I wouldn't do anything to hurt him and she said, "This is my boyfriend." He straightened up and said that he was sorry and that he didn't know. I thought to myself, I wonder what makes him think that that type of talk is okay, unless, they talk like this on a regular basis. When I asked her about it, she made it seem like it was nothing, but I couldn't shake my conscience on the situation.

I didn't trust her after this and we ended up breaking up in August 31st of 2015.

I tried to date again shortly after breakup to take my mind off things and the memories that we once shared. It was weird not having her apart of my life as we talked every night. Once again, I got on a dating app and found a date.

The date was extremely promiscuous and basically invited herself back to my place after we went to see a movie. For the first time in my life after turning 18, I actually turned down a woman that I wanted. I felt free from the cycle that I was used to, free to make my own choices. I even called my brother to tell him about it. Up until that time, it had felt like I had no choice but to continue going down the path of the cycle that I was stuck in. I later learned that this is called bondage.

Instead of filling my time with pursuing women, I decided to fill my time by making a commitment to read my Bible everyday. In my younger years, I remember watching my dad sit on his bed and read the Bible. He told me that he had a Bible reading plan and that he used it to read through the Bible year after year. I told myself that I would do that and I was also excited to see what would happen. I had already been experiencing God in my life and watched Him do things for me without me reading the Bible and having a close relationship with him.

I was curious to know what would happen if I got closer to Him by reading His word on a consistent basis. It was time to get with the program and be intentional concerning my growth with the Father.

THE PROMISE

After some time passed, Frank let me know over the phone that his cancer had returned after being in remission for a while. While he was previously in stage four with the cancer spreading to his liver, his theory was that because the doctors had not cut away the dead cancer cells this caused his cancer to come back. When the cancer came back, it was more aggressive and when they began chemotherapy. This time it was very taxing on his body.

I came back for Christmas vacation in 2015 and going to see Frank was my first stop as soon as I left the airport. As soon as I pulled up at the driveway, he came outside to greet me. Immediately, I could tell that he wasn't himself. He had lost weight and the weight that he did have didn't look proportioned as it once was. When I came in to give him a hug I could feel the tube in his chest where the chemotherapy was being administered. I began to feel a little uneasy as I had never seen him like this before. He was always so strong and full of life and energy, this wasn't the Frank that I knew.

I came in, sat down on his sofa, and I was so excited to talk about the Word that I just began asking questions concerning some of the things that I was reading. I had so many questions. He had a big bookshelf and as he sat down, he pointed to a specific book for me to pull down off of the shelf. The book was titled *How To Read The Bible For All Its Worth* by Gordon D. Fee and Douglas Stuart. He answered a few of my questions and read a few snippets of the book. After we got done talking about the book, I grabbed it and was about to put it back on the shelf where I got it from when he said, "No, I want you to take that with you." I began to tear up slightly because I got the sense - through the tone of his voice - that he was giving me the book because he knew that he wasn't going to be around for much longer on this earth.

I sat down as tears rolled down my face. While sitting he said, "I want you to know that you were my best student."

I looked at him, shocked that he said that to me. He had been teaching people since his teenage years and over that amount of time, he had over 5,000 students. I was curious and asked, "Why do you say that? How is that possible? You had students that could fight way better than me and had more skill than me." He responded with, "Yes, that's true. But you moved toward the Father." Instantly, I had a knowing that Frank wasn't just teaching people how to fight with wisdom filled lessons that could also be applied to life. He was using his fighting classes as a way to bring people in, so that He could minister to them. I didn't realize this until I had actually gotten into the Word for myself.

Some of the quotes that Frank would say were directly from the Bible, he just wouldn't say that they were in the moment. He was speaking life into each and every student that came through those doors. Many of the students were not receptive to some of his blatant teachings of the Word, but Frank never compromised.

We sat there talking for a little while longer and he gestured for me to bring him another book that was sitting on his computer desk. The book was titled, The *Leadership Secrets Of Jesus* by Mike Murdock. There was a binder of the notes that Frank had taken after going through the entire Bible as he was preparing to go into ministry years ago. With the binder in mind he kept beating himself up saying, "Man, I wish I could have gotten that binder to you filled with all of my notes." He was shaking his head in disappointment, but I continued crying and listening as his words only confirmed that he knew that he had run out of time.

One of Frank's other students called to check on him while we were talking and he also wanted to talk to me. I picked up the phone and we talked for a little while. At the end of the phone call, he said, "I need for you to pray for that man." I told him that I would, and when I got off the phone, I grabbed Frank's hands in prayer. He was receiving of the prayer at first, but then he opened up his eyes, smiled, and stopped me from praying. He said, "Nah, let me pray for you." As he said this, he began to cry, it was the first time that I had ever seen Frank cry. When he began to pray, the only thing that I remember was him saying "... and lead him (me) to the perfection of ministry."

I remember thinking to myself, how could I ever be used to do something so great? But then my faith kicked in to let me know that all things are possible to those who believe (Mark 9:23).

After the prayer, we continued talking for a while, mostly about the Lord. Then Frank brought up one of his favorite topics of the Bible, running the race (Heb 12:1-3). I knew that it was one of his favorites because he talked about it so often and the passion that came over him when he talked about it made anyone listening want to smile. His face would light up as he spoke about how things would get tough, but we have to continue pressing toward the mark of the high call (Phil 3:14). We have to fight at times and move toward things in life that make us feel uncomfortable, humbling ourselves before the Lord and believing no matter how tough the situation may seem. His eyes lit up and he was smiling as he spoke. It really motivated me to move closer to God.

Before I knew it, I had been at Frank's house almost the entire day. It was coming close to the time for me to leave, we hugged for a while and he said to me, "Run the race."

I promised him that I would. As I was opening the door to leave, he held his finger up to make a point and said, "Always remember this, read the Bible first before anything. The books that I have given you and any book that you will read in the future are but supplements to the Word. The Word is the source of all things, it is the foundation by which everything was and still is created." I told him that I would and opened the door to leave. I cried all the way to my mother's house, which is where I was staying for this particular Christmas vacation.

The next day, I linked up with my brother and we went to go see the movie Creed, which had just come out in the theaters. The movie was great, and it hit me harder than I expected. Sylvester Stallone's character in the movie had cancer and he was the trainer of Adonis Creed in the movie. It was like I was living that life and literally watching it on the screen. Frank was my trainer, my teacher, my coach, and my mentor. He had been battling cancer for about two years at this point. There were so many emotions pulsating through my body at the time that I couldn't contain them. I began crying, balling if you will, right there next to my brother. At that moment, I began preparing for what was about to happen. I began preparing myself mentally for the possibility that Frank would pass on to see the Father, or the true Master, as Frank would say.

I went back to see Frank two days later, I wanted to make sure that I soaked up as much time with him while he was still living. I went over to his house and there were a few other students there. Frank was still teaching classes and correcting people on form. I joined in on the Tai Chi class and did some light sparring with one of the students afterwards. Mostly everyone left after class, but another student and I hung around to soak up more time with Frank. We ordered some food and just talked for a few hours, laughing and cracking jokes.

Then it was time for Frank to take his medication, and when he did, he got lethargic. We thought that it would be best for us to leave so that he could get some rest, so we did.

When it came time for me to leave Georgia, I dropped my rental car off at the airport and waited for my flight. I couldn't help but to think about Frank. He had taught me so much in the seven years that I knew him, how could I not think about him in the state that he was in? I ended up crying all the way back to Oklahoma while listening to If I Fight, You Fight from the Creed soundtrack, preparing myself for what he and I both knew would happen. I sent him a text on the 29th of Dec., 2015, asking him how he was feeling. He replied back with, "Very bad, but God's got me."

THE WAKE-UP CALL

On Jan. 1st, 2016, I received a message on Facebook Messenger from one of Frank's other students who still lived in Georgia. It read, "Give me a call as soon as you can." I already knew what this meant and I was prepared to hear it. I gave the other student a call and he said in a sad tone, "Well, Frank passed away early this morning." We continued to talk for a little while, talking about when the funeral would be and how weird it would be not having him to talk to. I told him, "It was time to stand up strong and push forward no matter how hard life became. Frank was a great man, but he was just that - a man. The most important thing for us to realize about Frank and anyone in the Word is that the people weren't great, it was the Lord working through them that made them great! We saw the light of Christ through Frank and that's what made him who he was." He told me about how Frank was the one giving him advice and basically keeping him out of the gutters of life. I identified with this in the aspect of not going directly to the Lord when I had questions, instead, I went to Frank. But now that Frank was gone and I realized that it was the Lord all along that was using Frank to teach me, it was time for me to go to the Lord fully with everything and I ended up giving this particular student the same advice.

GOING BUCK-WILD IN CHRIST

After I hung up the phone with him, I sat at the edge of my bed and spoke to the Lord. I said to Him, "Thank you Lord for sending me a mentor, teacher, and friend like Frank. I ask that You allow him to hear me when I say this, I promise both of you that I will run this race and do my best. Frank, I will run this race! Thank you, Lord." I sat there for a minute, thinking about all of the good times that we shared together.

It seems like you remember much more of what the person has said in the past when you no longer have them to talk to anymore. I contemplated taking the week off of the gym - as I began bodybuilding in February of 2015 - allowing myself time to mourn his death. But then I thought about it, he wouldn't want me slowing down, he would want me speeding up and being intentional about my walk and relationship with the Lord as well as ministering to people about the Word and what the Lord was teaching me. I didn't have time to mourn, I would have to just mourn on the go!

As I sat there, I began to become righteously angry about my dealings with the Lord, people, and my personal walk with Him. I had wasted so much time pursuing women for the wrong purposes, and power - all things that didn't matter. I hadn't been bold in my walk with the Lord and at times even allowed people to sway my opinion about the Lord based on their non-Biblical beliefs. I was too afraid to share my faith because of what I thought people might think.

I was too afraid to combat people in confrontations, concerning why Jesus doesn't exist and how whatever people believe we really all believe in the same "thing" because I didn't want to stand out and tell people the truth - that Jesus is the only way. I was too afraid of walking alone on this journey and would allow people and women into my life that were just there to waste my time and pull me from the spiritual growth, through relationship, that I had the potential of experiencing. Why was it that I was able to talk to anyone, especially random pretty women, about sex but I wasn't able to talk to people in general about the most important person that has ever walked this earth? WHY?!

I was afraid of being criticized and ostracized from people that I liked, from places that I frequented, and from women that I was attracted to... No more!

From this point on, I didn't care whether people wanted to hear the Word preached or not, they were going to hear it. I didn't care whether people liked hearing Jesus brought up in conversation or not, He was getting brought up. I didn't care where people were located when I was ministering to them, whether they were at family gatherings, at work, working at restaurants, at Walmart, or even in the restroom stall beside me - they were going to hear about Jesus. I didn't care whether the Word of God was warranted or not, whether people liked me anymore after talking about Him or not - I already had it set in my mind that people weren't going to like me anyway because the world never liked Jesus.

The bottom line is that I came to the realization that the Word of God is an active word, it is living, and anything that is living is always in motion in some way. This motion can be displayed in something as simple as a living plant that is growing or a person that simply has a heartbeat.

Because this is the case, I realized that it's important for us to not only read the Word, but to start doing it. By this time I had heard so many Christians say, "I didn't minister to that person, because I didn't feel led to or because I didn't have instruction to." But the Lord has already given us instruction in His Word, He told us to go into all the world and preach the gospel to all creation (Mark 16:15). I wasn't going to wait anymore or make up anymore excuses, I was going to go buck-wild for Christ, actually putting this word in motion as it is designed to be - and I didn't care whether people hated me for it. There were no excuses, I was just going to be obedient and leave the rest up to Him.

As I began walking with the Lord, passionately filling myself up by reading the Word and intentionally trying to release everything that He was filling me with into the people that surrounded me, I began to notice a few things. I began to see churches that were more concerned about church attendance than actually building up the body of Christ to stand strong, equipping them with theology as well as spiritual understanding. They had turned the church into more of a business than being used to release the power of the Almighty, All Knowing, All Powerful God - Jesus Christ. I have met with pastors that think that it's okay to have racist sermons preached at their church, trying to sway the congregation into believing that it is right to think that way, as if racism is beyond the realm of forgiveness concerning African Americans and that we are entitled to think that way.

I have heard of churches that do not want sermons containing the blood of Jesus Christ preached to their congregation. I began to see Christians that were moving in religion, thinking that they could somehow earn the love of Christ through their actions, as if what He did on the cross wasn't enough. I also began to see Christians judging newer Christians as if we are supposed to be perfect as soon as they become saved, that's not the case, and everyone has a past. It was like all of a sudden I became so sensitive to things that I could have cared less about when I wasn't walking alongside Christ before.

I began to go out and practice hearing God's voice. I knew what He sounded like when He was speaking to me through people, but I wanted to be spot on in hearing Him when He was speaking to me directly. I would go to Walmart and look at people, asking Him to give me a message for them or to tell me something about them while I was already walking toward them.

I didn't care if I was wrong concerning speaking what I thought I heard Him say, I needed to practice hearing the Lord in all facets of His speaking. Whether that was pictures in my mind's eye, immediate thought impressions after asking Him a question, or even words that are impressed upon me.

When I came to the realization that none of this was about me and that it was all about God, it took the pressure off of me to care about what other people thought. If they had a problem, then that was their problem and a reflection of their character, not mine. Regardless, I didn't care where the people were located, they were going to hear about Jesus that day.

WHAT ARE YOU LISTENING TO?

During this time period, one of my favorite places to minister was the gym. A lot of the people there were Christians, so it was relatively easy to minister to people that wanted to know more about God, anyway.

Though, most of the people that went to this particular gym weren't living passionately for the Lord, He was using my passion to ignite a fire within people to desire the God that I had, the God that wasn't being preached very often. Most Christians learn about a Jesus in church that has all of this power, yet the way that they are being taught is such that they can apply principles from the Word to their lives without ever getting to know Him - versus reading the Word for themselves to develop a relationship, submitting their will to Him, and then watching Him work in their lives. There is no power being released, because there is no relationship with Him.

On February 3rd, 2016, I was working legs and as I was walking to one of the machines, I noticed a girl with her earphones on. She did a funny dance to the music she was listening to and I stopped in my tracks, stared with a smile on my face, and laughed once she looked up to acknowledge that she saw me staring. After I finished using the machine, I walked over to her and asked, "What are you listening to? It must be good if it has you dancing like that." We both had a little laugh and she proceeded to hand me her sweaty earphones.

I looked at her in disgust, as I wasn't expecting her to hand them to me sweaty, I just wanted her to tell me the name of the song. I took the earphones with two fingers, making sure that I didn't allow them to touch the rest of my body and held them just close enough to my face to hear a crappy rap song with no lyrical content. We talked for a bit and then I headed home.

The next day, I came in and she approached me. I had totally forgotten her name, but before the night was over, I began to minister to her as she was on the treadmill. I told her funny stories about my life involving the Lord, as well as some of the things that He taught me. She told me a little about her life and how both of her parents had committed suicide. She was on the brink of tears as she spoke and she was surprised that she was. I told her that I don't have the power to make people cry, and that the Lord may be touching her heart with our stories and vulnerability. I asked her if she was saved and she told me that she was. I asked if she had a Bible and she told me that she did, so I told her that I would have something for her soon.

Eventually, I brought her a Bible reading plan and we began to talk on a more consistent basis. Sometimes we would go out to my car after a workout for a short talk, which ended up lasting for hours. She was fun to talk to, but she wasn't a strong Christian and basic things that I felt all Christians should know, she had no understanding of. She struggled with her belief in the Lord, and I could identify with that so I took it upon myself to help her. I didn't realize it at the time, but I had a strong messiah complex, thinking that I could help people, even save them from their problems. Little did I know that this girl would be used to teach me a powerful lesson of the Lord after she became my girlfriend.

There were a lot of red flags with her in the beginning. She hung out with people that weren't going anywhere in their life and just drank, smoked, and complained. There's a saying, "Tell me who your friends are and I'll tell you who you are." This is who she was at the time. But what sparked me was the potential for greatness that I saw in her. She smoked cigarettes and marijuana, but one day as I was riding in the car with her, she pulled out a cigarette to smoke.

As she did, I said to her, "Usually people who smoke cigarettes are under a lot of stress and smoke to take the edge off - a pacifier, if you will. You don't need that, you're better than that." She immediately looked at me and threw the cigarettes away and never smoked again. She stopped cold turkey right there in the moment and I thought to myself that I could teach this girl so much!

THE CHANGE IN MYSELF

Because she was so fun, and we were spending more time together for a few months, over time I began to become sexually attracted to her whereas before I didn't see her that way at all. We began having sex and I immediately felt a change in my passion for the Lord, it almost physically hurt me to have sex at this point in my life. Now that my relationship with the Lord was stronger than it had ever been, I could feel that battle that was going on internally with my spirit and my carnal desires. I had been walking alongside the Lord for a while and sinning actually began to hurt.

After having sex with her, there would be times where I would take time off from the gym and go on a fast to be lifted up in the Lord and to humble myself before Him (James 4:10). Having sex for her was a normal thing to do in a relationship, it was like she didn't know any better. Slowly but surely, we continued having sex and after a while I noticed that I felt too ashamed to minister to people. I began to slowly think in my old mindset and I felt like I was dying on the inside.

Sex was debilitating me and she didn't seem to be affected by it, not even in the slightest.

THE BACK AND FORTH

My Bible reading began to slow down in terms of passion and I always felt like I was in a position to constantly have to choose between her and the Lord. Everything in my life seemed to be in disarray as I spent most of my time with her. We argued quite often with her constantly challenging and going against everything that came out of my mouth concerning the Lord. I would end up breaking up with her and then getting back in a relationship with her because of the guilt that I felt when I left her on her own. Satan was so good at making me feel guilty for leaving her where she was, though I knew this was the right thing to do. I didn't know it was Satan working in the background at the time, there were thoughts that would invade my mind, "If you don't help her, who will? You're her light, the one who can show her the way." So, I would go back. I didn't know it, but I was being weakened more and more each time I did. I wasn't taking care of my own priorities, instead all my focus was on her to build her up, teach her, and be her "savior" in the midst of darkness. I had this mindset the entire time and it was a vicious cycle of breaking up to make up, filled with poisonous cocktails of arguments that were all rooted in her unbelief. But I would stick around, thinking that I could change her. The Lord would have to free me and help me through this, as I felt so drained and didn't feel I was strong enough to drop her.

CALL TO ACTION

Once we have gotten serious and have decided to take Christ's hand in acceptance and responsibility to our calling and His universal commands, there is a time period of growth and development that is vital. We are always in a state of learning from the Lord, but the beginning stages can seem like some of the toughest ones, as we are transitioning into a different way of life. Walking boldly and unapologetically may seem scary and it is easy to just come home, read the Bible, and not openly be obedient to His commands in fear of the thoughts of others. If you would like to begin your bold walk into the unknown, pray the below prayer AND be prepared to take a step.

"Lord, I desire to be a walking representation of You at all times. But sometimes I live in fear of what other people think. I ask that you shock me into boldness in such a way that will light an undying fire of passion that engulfs my fear. Help me to begin to stand and walk boldly as an ambassador of love and relationship with You. Help me to remain bold, even in the darkest of times. Amen."

CHAPTER 4

I HEAR YOU KNOCKING

One day, in November of 2016, after coming back home from the gym, eating, and going to sleep, I began to hear a knocking sound. It woke me up out of my sleep. At first, I couldn't tell if I was hearing the knocks in a dream or if they were actually in my house. It startled me so much that I sat up in my bed to listen more closely to see if I could hear it again. I heard it again, and it was four knocks on my bedroom door. I sat there frozen in bed, hoping that whatever it was wouldn't try to come into my room. I was imagining myself fighting someone or something and being forced to defend myself. At that point, I wouldn't wish that on anybody.

As I continued listening, courage came over me and I got out of bed and tiptoed to the door to listen more closely. For some reason, I just knew instinctively that whatever this was, wasn't human.

I listened from inside my bedroom as it shuffled papers around in the office area right outside of my bedroom. I then heard its footsteps go down my stairs and knock on my front door, as if to say "bye-bye."

I stood there frozen for about thirty minutes. I was intently listening to see if there were anymore sounds or indications that it was still there. I felt I had a chance if it was a human, but I didn't know the slightest thing to do if it was a demon. At the time, I hadn't heard of spiritual warfare and if it decided to come into my room, I wouldn't have known how to fight. Spiritual warfare was an undiscovered category in my life at this point.

The next night it happened again, except this time it seemed to be more aggressive, as if it wanted me to know that it was there. I heard the four knocks on my bedroom door, except this time it sounded like it was accompanied by scratches on the wall beside my bedroom. I sat there just trying to take all of this in. Then I noticed that there might be two of whatever type of demon it was because there were knocks on my door as well as shuffling of papers in the office area outside of my bedroom.

This went on for about 15 minutes until everything just suddenly stopped. My heart was racing and it was terrifying to even move. I mustered up courage and opened the door this time, there was nothing there that I could see. I didn't see any markings on the wall, and even though I heard shuffling of papers in my office area, there was nothing that was out of place. I was baffled by this and turned around to go back to sleep.

Things went on like this for a few months. The demonic presence would enter my home at around 3 a.m. in the morning. I would hear the same things described previously with the exception of sometimes hearing the first four knocks inside of my bedroom (sometimes on my headboard). With everything going on, I knew I needed some help. I called my grandmother once again, I knew that she had a deep relationship with the Lord and knew about spiritual warfare. She asked me if I had ever prayed over my house and anointed it. I told her that I didn't know what any of that meant. She went on to explain to me that praying over your home keeps the atmosphere in your home guarded against the forces of darkness and open to the kingdom of heaven.

I got off the phone with her, still not really knowing what I needed to do next or what steps I needed to take in order to fight against the demonic forces in my home, I was confused.

One morning, the Lord invaded my thoughts and told me to look up how to spiritually clean your house.

I was led to *Protecting Your Home From Spiritual Darkness* by Chuck Pierce. I did some research on the book to make sure that it wouldn't lead me in the wrong direction. I didn't want to follow the teachings of a false prophet or someone that didn't believe what I believed about our Savior. I ended up buying the book. I immediately began reading and was amazed to find out that there were many similar stories like what I was going through concerning dark forces scaring people in their houses. I was excited to implement the steps of prayer and applications of faith outlined in the book.

WHY ARE YOU SO INTERESTED IN SEEING?

In the first week of January of 2017, my cousin was going to get married. Instead of coming back for Christmas, I decided that I would save the vacation time for that year and come back for the wedding to see everybody then. My grandmother was staying at my dad's house and that's where I was going to be staying as well. I woke up one morning and as I was eating breakfast with her, she brought up the knocking situation to get more details about it. She then told me about how she had prayed over her home with oil and applied it to every door, entrance, window, and every possible way that someone could enter her house. Then she proceeded to plead the blood of Jesus around her house with the Lord's guidance and direction. I remember being somewhat skeptical of the "pleading the blood of Jesus" part. I was struggling to find the Biblical basis for it. The Lord began to teach me about the power of His blood and how we were saved by it, we were redeemed by it, and delivered by it. I realized that my grandma was applying the principles of the blood to the spiritual atmosphere around her house as a form of protection. The oil was a representation of the blood of Jesus and provides protection in the same way it did in the passover, Exodus 12:13:

> The blood will be a sign for you on the houses where you are, and when I see the blood, I will pass over you. No destructive plague will touch you when I strike Egypt.

We all got dressed and made our way to the wedding, which was being held in a rented venue in downtown Atlanta. Everyone came dressed up and ready to see my cousin walk down the aisle with her new husband. As I walked in, I noticed that everyone was scrambling to make sure that everything would be perfect for my cousin's wedding day. I was excited because I hadn't been to many weddings in my life, unless one were to count me being the ring bearer and smelling the pillow that the ring came on as I walked down the aisle at 4 years old. At this wedding, they had a DJ, a dance floor, alcohol, food, a photo booth, and singers for the father daughter dance. I had only seen this in movies and couldn't wait to let loose like a dancing fool, while recording the whole experience.

I ended up taking plenty of pictures with my grandmother and uncle at the photobooth and making people laugh with my 80s popping and locking dancing skills. It was an amazing night with family and meeting new people.

On the ride back home from the wedding, I asked my step-mom if she had ever seen any spirits. I loved hearing those types of stories, whether they were scary or not. It was so interesting to me to be able to see things that aren't normally seen. She said that she had many spiritual experiences in her past.

She proceeded to tell a story about a cousin of hers that had gotten possessed and became incredibly strong. The police were called in on her cousin and she became so strong that she threw the policeman off of her as if they were toddlers. She was running around naked at the time and after the police finally detained her, all that the police could talk about was the way that her eyes looked. Her cousin ended up in a psych ward, never to be heard of again.

After my step-mom finished her story my dad asked me, "Why are you so interested in spiritual things?" I told him that it has always been something that I wanted to do and have always found it fascinating when people would tell me stories of the things that they would see or had seen. Then I proceeded to tell a story of something that Frank saw when he was 14 years old. He said that he was sitting by the window, just looking at the clouds and thinking about the Lord when suddenly huge white horses began galloping through the sky.

He began to scream in excitement, asking his brother who was sitting beside him, ""Do you see that?! Do you see that?!" The horses ran past their house and Frank mentioned that they were the size of a small building.

I smiled as I told the story, literally visualizing myself there to experience such a new, fascinating thing of God. My dad then proceeded to tell me stories about my great grandmother and her spiritual sight. I ate it up and was thrilled at the possibility of one day being able to see myself.

It came time for my trip to end and I was completely ready to implement some of the things that my grandmother and I talked about. When I got back home, I began to read the Chuck Pierce book again. He outlined very well the step-by-step battle plan to rid your home from any type of spiritual darkness. The first thing that I did was pray over the land that my townhouse sat on. I didn't know what had taken place in the past, but I asked the Lord to reveal it to me as I prayed over it.

I asked forgiveness for the sinful things that had taken place there. I then proceeded to go around my house as many times as the Lord led, pleading the blood of Jesus. I ended up doing it three times. Then, the book instructed me to use oil as I prayed. Oil is a representation of the blood of Jesus and should be put over every entrance to my house.

I did so, and immediately realized that the book was saying - in more detail - almost exactly what my grandmother was saying when I spoke with her. The Lord was instructing me and confirming through the book what my grandmother had said. The book then instructed me to pray over each room based on the activity that is supposed to take place there. For example, if I were praying over the kitchen I would pray over the meals that would be produced there and ask the Lord to bless every soul that ingests the meals. After doing this, I never heard the knocks or the office paper shuffling or the scratches on the wall again.

My house felt peaceful and I was excited to see what the Lord was going to do in my life afterwards. The presence of darkness and demonic visitations were gone!

FREEDOM FROM PORN & MASTURBATION

As I began to grow in my spiritual awareness, I became aware of things in my life that were happening physically that were really spiritual battles. One of those battles was with porn and masturbation. I'd really like to tell you that I am a perfect Christian, but the reality is that just isn't the case, nor will it be for any of us.

What I am about to reveal to you is something that I had been struggling with ever since I was 12 years old. The struggle with porn and masturbation did not end for me until 15 years later, at the age of 27. I am sharing the testimony in hopes that it will be used to set you free as well, I hope that the Lord uses my openness and vulnerability to release the same power used to break my addiction and the hold of perversion once and for all in your life, if this is your struggle as well. Most of us would like to keep this a secret, but I find that bringing these things up to the surface doesn't allow Satan to have any place to hide in your life and is the first step in the Lord taking it from you, if you are ready to fully let go of it.

There I was, it was mid-day on a Sunday and I was getting sexual desires and imagery in my mind and even replaying some of the sexual encounters I had in the past. It became so extreme to me that I reached for my laptop, turned it on, and proceeded to look at porn. I felt so dirty.

For the first time in my life, I realized that I couldn't stop even if I tried, I had been living in denial about it since the time I started.

The longest I had been able to go was about two weeks without masturbating and then I was right back to it with the accompaniment of sex with multiple partners or a girlfriend. After coming to the realization that I couldn't stop, I began to cry. Tears came down my face in shame and regret for allowing myself to partake in such an evil thing for as long as I had been doing it.

I began to cry out to the Lord, I didn't care how ugly I looked at the time, whether snot was coming out of my nose, or if spit was coming out of my mouth. I wanted to be free and I was willing to scream and squirm until it happened. I spoke out loud, "Lord I have tried to stop on my own so many times, for years I have tried! I can't do it on my own, Lord. I need you to take this away from me. Please send me help, Lord. Please send me help!" Periodically throughout the rest of the day tears ran down my face and I continued to ask Him as much as I could think of it, "Lord, please send me help."

When I was asking for help, I had the picture in my mind of Him sending me to some type of 12 step program. The next morning I jumped out of bed! I was normally always sluggish and tired, but on this day things were different, something had changed, I knew it and I could feel it. I got in the shower to get ready for work and I asked the Lord, smiling, "What did you do?! I know you did something! I feel amazing. It was like I didn't desire anything sexual and it feels like a weight has been lifted off of me." I kept asking God throughout the day, but I didn't get my answer until that night in my Bible reading. At the time I was using a Bible reading plan to read through the Bible in a year. One of the verses that it had me read was Psalm 34:17 (AMP), which reads:

```
"When the righteous cry [for
help], the Lord hears. And rescues
them from all their distress
and troubles."
```

This was the Lord answering my question. He was letting me know that He set me free because I had asked for help and was serious about it. At the time of asking for help, I knew nothing of this verse and wasn't claiming it to be set free, all I knew was that I wanted to be set free. I meant it with the entirety of my being, and He did it!

CALL TO ACTION

When you recognize your struggle and see that it is not only flesh and blood, but spiritual (Eph. 6:12). Then you can engage in crying out to the Lord in intervention for your freedom. One thing to note, for most people freedom is not a one and done type of thing. Satan will still be coming after you. It is important that we develop spiritual practices, discipline, and our relationship with God to maintain this freedom. For me, this has been the reality. It's not that I'm not tempted anymore, I am. It's that I have developed the discipline, spiritual practices, and boundaries to fight back and keep the door closed to Satan. If you are ready to fight for your freedom, say the below prayer.

"In the name of Jesus, I close every door to Satan and perversion. It has no place in my life and I repent for having opened the door in the beginning. Lord place a hedge of protection around my thought life, my soul, and my desires. Help me to constantly think holy thoughts and thoughts that glorify your kingdom. I claim Psalm 34:17, and I am crying out to you. I need you, Lord. Please send me help. Amen."

....

CHAPTER 5
SPIRITUAL EYES OPENED

While at work on the same day, after the Lord revealed to me what he did, I was looking for another spiritual book that I could read to give me the "how to" components of praying and watching the Lord defeat the enemy. I had already seen His power in its entirety when He took that demon out of my house. Curiosity got the best of me, I wanted more of Him and I wanted to experience the full expression of Him. I got onto Amazon to look for more books. There were many books that were recommended to me because I had bought Chuck Pierce's book.

There were only two books that grabbed my attention. These books were Michael Van Vlylmen's books titled *How To See In The Spirit* and *Supernatural Travel*. I've always had the desire to see what others could not and to do what others could not and would not. It was almost as if I was being called to it.

The desire was always there, I just didn't know what to do about it. Before I knew it, my mouse rested on the books and I was looking inside, as Amazon gives you the great option of doing so. To my surprise, there was a prayer in the *Supernatural Transportation book*. I remember thinking to myself, if he's going to give away the goodies, I'll definitely take them! I read the prayer under my breath, which read:

```
"Father in heaven, I call upon the
resources of heaven. I call upon
the angelic armies to minister your
perfect will in my household. Let
the angels of the Lord manifest
their presence and their power
openly in my home. Let the men in
white linen, the living creatures,
and the cloud of witnesses minister
your will to my household. Let your
light and your glory fill this place
to overflowing."
```

After reading this, I went about my business and didn't really think that it could be as simple as just saying a prayer to begin seeing in the spirit. But, I continued to read every little snippet of every book Michael had out there. I took all of the "freebies" without actually having to commit to buying the book. He talked about things that I had never heard before, coming from a background of going to a Baptist church.

He seemed to have personal relationships with angels and even knew some of them by name. They taught him things and took him on spiritual adventures outside of the body. They joked with him and wrestled with him in his bed. They actually laughed as if they had human characteristics. He told stories of watching angels smack demons around as if it were child's play. My imagination ran wild with each snippet of every one of his books that I read. I had a tab open for every book and at this point, I was fully engaged and hung onto every word of those books.

I did the same thing the next day, which was the day that my eyes were opened.

The next day after I got home from work I realized something felt different. I had left worship music on at home all day. I was on the phone with my girlfriend at the time and I raised my hands in praise and told her that my house felt completely different and how I could feel movement around me without being able to see it.

It was the type of movement that one feels if they were to close their eyes and have someone else move their hand in front of the person with their eyes closed. The movement doesn't make a sound, but you can feel that it is there without actually being able to see it. She was perplexed by this and seemed jealous that I was beginning to experience things out of the ordinary after saying the prayer. I changed the topic and we continued talking as I got ready for the gym. For some reason, on this particular day she wasn't going to join me at the gym. I told her that if I saw the guy at the gym that badmouthed me, that I would go up to him and ask him to forgive me for lashing out at him. I didn't want anything hindering my spiritual growth with the Lord and if something as simple as forgiveness was all I needed to do, then I was going to do it.

The bad mouthing scenario started a while back after I had broken up with the girlfriend that I was with at the time. She didn't have wifi at her house, so she went to the gym one weekend to work on some personal projects of her own. This particular gym had a seating area in the front with leather sofas and she was sitting there typing.

This guy, Larry, approached her and began a conversation. She listened to him but wasn't interested in the conversation. He let her know how amazingly pretty she was and how she seemed like she could hold really good conversation.

He also let her know that he was married with a few kids and asked her if she had a boyfriend. She told him that she didn't have a boyfriend - because I had just broken up with her - but she was interested in someone that went to the gym. He inquired and asked who that was and when she responded with "he's the bodybuilder that you see around here, you know, the guy that is always talking to everybody about God," he flipped. He spat out his true malice that he had for me and said "That guy? What are you gonna do with a little pretty puppy like that? He can't please you. Plus, he has a tainted image of what and who God really is. Jesus isn't real, He was forced on black people when white people kept us as slaves. Your little puppy needs to do his research." She sat there listening as he continued with his little rant of jealousy.

He tried to give her a history lesson that was all based on racist imagery, painting the picture that white people are the source of all black people problems. He continued further and tried to pull on her emotional strings by stating that he has been beaten by white cops in the past, how he's wanted to kill himself in the past, and how she seemed like she could be someone that he could talk to. He ended the conversation by giving her his number and walking out of the gym. She told me about all of this, and because I had lived in a manipulative atmosphere almost all my life, it was easy for me to recognize his manipulation in this conversation.

Satan tries to manipulate us in this way as well in our society. He wants to sway us into thinking a certain way, providing false "proven" evidence on television, our phones, in music, and in certain communities to win us over into believing more in us and what we can do in our own power without God.

Satan uses suggestive speech and imagery in commercials and in movies to desensitize us into believing that these things are the norm and that we should accept them if we are to be accepted in the world.

One of the biggest of these movements has been homosexuality, and some Christians even believe that it is in conjunction with the spirit of the anti-Christ or is the anti-Christ. Christians, don't get me wrong, we are to wholeheartedly love all people and there is no sin that is greater than any other sin - stealing a piece of candy carries the same weight as fornication, adultery, etc. - but we do have a responsibility to stay strong in the Word and tell people the truth regardless of whether people like it or not. We do this in a loving way, not condemning them, but addressing the issue to motivate them and allowing them to make their own choices. I had to learn that myself!

After she told me all that he said, I initially laughed everything off, but the more I thought about it, the angrier I became. My initial anger started when I recognized all of the manipulative techniques that he was trying to use to get her to budge. Then my anger rose to another level when I thought about how much of a baby she was in the faith and how he may have been trying to take advantage of that by spewing racist doctrine on her in such an abrupt way. I wanted to defend her, I wanted to stand up for her and stand between her and harm's way.

The last straw was when I thought about how he was talking about me and if he really felt this way, why wasn't he man enough to come and say it to my face rather than talking to a woman about me? I had ministered to him about the Lord in the past, so he knew exactly who I was.

I decided that the next time I saw him, I would confront him about it and talk man to man. On this particular day my girlfriend and I were excited for the workout and to teach her specific movements of each exercise and the muscles incorporated.

As we approached the gym, I could see him through the window coming out of the gym. He began to walk out and held the door open for us. She walked in first, but I proceeded to put my stuff down on the concrete sidewalk area in front of the gym. I pointed at him, and directed my question toward her, "this is him, right?" She nodded her head and it was on. I then turned to him and asked, "So what is this I hear about you talking behind my back? Do you have something that you want to say to me? Because I'm here now."

By this time she had walked outside and was looking upon the situation with fear. Larry proceeded to speak, "What are you talking about?" Then looked at her and asked, "What is he talking about?" She proceeded to speak fearfully and he cut her off and stated that he and I should probably talk and let her go on and workout. She went inside and I was ready to fight without getting his side of the story.

"Do you have something you would like to say to me? I don't have to go behind anyone's back to talk about them, I go directly to the source of the problem if I have something to say."

He looked at me slightly in fear and said that he didn't. I proceeded to talk, "What kind of a married man with kids goes and tries to flirt with anyone?! You're supposed to be the example of what a real man is, not only in a relationship, but in society. You are supposed to set the standard!" He looked at me and said, "My wife and I have an open relationship, plus I was trying to leave and your girl wanted to continue talking." I thought to myself that one of them is lying and I don't deal with liars. I realized that this was going to be about him playing the blame game and not taking responsibility for anything that he said or apparently didn't say.

I changed the topic to Christianity and asked, "What is it that you believe? She told me that you stated that Christianity is a religion that was forced upon black people, which isn't true. There is evidence in Ethiopia, Africa that proves that black people were worshiping Jesus long before any European influence."

He looked at me and I could tell that he didn't have anything to combat that, he wasn't prepared for a Christian that actually knew the Word and a little bit of the history behind it. All that he said was, "I was just trying to inform her, but you're over here trying to tear down what others believe." I fired back, "That's just the thing, I still don't know what you believe. If someone were to ask me what I believe, I could easily tell them that I believe that Jesus died on the cross for my sins and I believe Him to be the one true God and the only way to get to heaven." He started, "Well, you would have to do research to understand what I believe, I can't just tell you.

"Are you willing to come to any meetings?" I let him know that I wasn't willing to come to any meetings thinking to myself that he could be a part of some type of racist cult that has Satan as the Godhead. I wanted no part of it.

After our long and drawn out conversation outside, I gave him another chance to be a man and own up to what I knew he said, "Do you have anything that you would like to say to me?" He said, "No." Then proceeded to try to calm me down by saying, "You know, sometimes girls will lie when they really like you and you're not paying them enough attention." I just remained quiet and when he extended his hand, I walked past him. Larry raised his voice behind me, "It's like that?" I responded, "It's like that." I walked inside and found her, she was sitting on a chair wondering what happened and thinking to herself that she should have never told me about the situation.

I asked her if she had lied to me about everything and she told me that she hadn't. I knew that if she had then I really owed this guy an engraved apology. I just went home after that, feeling good about myself for defending not only her and myself, but also Christianity. In the coming weeks at the gym, I ignored Larry and acted like he wasn't there. He had disgusted me on every level.

I had no respect for a man like that and I wasn't going to pretend like I did. This went on for about six months, until I realized that I was wrong for doing that and arrogant for believing that I was entitled to acting out the way that I did. I was ready to forgive, and when it came time to forgive, my entire life was never going to be the same.

On this particular day, I was ready and prepared to humble myself and do the very thing that God has told all of us to do, and that is to forgive. I walked into the gym and put my workout gear down and started toward the free weight section of the gym. Larry was standing in front of the mirror and looked as though he was about to pick up a dumbbell. I didn't waste any time, and started toward him. I approached him and asked, "Can I talk to you for a minute?" He said, "Sure." I started by saying, "I just need for you to forgive me, man. I was wrong for being resentful toward you and ignoring you around here. I'm sorry." After I said that he said, "You know what? I could feel that, man. I forgave you a long time ago and I respect you so much more. It takes a real man to come up and admit when he is wrong." He proceeded to talk about religion and stated, "If you really think about it, we all believe in the same God, you know?" I just looked at him and let him know that this is one thing that we will always disagree on.

After leaving the gym, I felt amazing. I showered, read the Bible, and just wound down. I cut off all of the lights in the rest of my house, except for my bedroom and proceeded to close my bedroom door and sit on the bed. While looking at my phone, out of my peripheral vision, I saw a see through armored leg of gold and silver standing right in front of my bedroom door. The leg was sparkling and I could see a little above the knee, yet I could still see my door behind it.

As a natural reflex, I looked up to get a better view of whatever was standing there but it disappeared as soon as I looked with my natural eyes and not in my peripheral vision. I sat there looking for a second and said out loud (because I had read in Michael Van Vlymen's book snippets that he was asking them their names) "I saw you! What is your name?!" I didn't hear anything and sat there still trying to look with my natural eyes for a second because I had the inkling that the angel was still there. I wondered to myself why he would disappear like that. Then I got up, turned off the light in my room, and got under the cover.

I was still looking at my phone when I saw a white ball of light positioned on my bathroom door about three feet away from my bed. I continued to look at my phone for a second so that I could continue to see the ball of light. After I couldn't take it anymore and wanted to see the ball of light in its full glory, I looked with my natural eyes and as soon as I did the ball disappeared.

I went to sleep and was about twenty minutes into sleeping when I heard a strong voice talking to me. It seemed to be coming from the edge of my bed. I couldn't make out what the voice was saying but it was so strong that it literally shook my insides. It sent my body on a natural reflex and I ended up jumping about six inches off of the bed, landing back on the bed with a crash. I opened my eyes and didn't see anything. I figured that it was the armored angel that I had seen trying to communicate with me, but I was so tired that I just spoke out loud and said, "Hey, I'm tired right now. I'll talk to you some other time." I didn't hear anything after this. Though, I figured that I would see him again.

It wasn't until later - after actually getting Michael's books - that I learned that when your spiritual eyes are beginning to open, you see out of your peripherals first. Then when your spiritual eyes are strengthened you see in both realms with your natural eyes and spiritual eyes at the same time.

After hearing the angels voice and seeing his leg, I asked the Lord what this angels name was. I genuinely wanted to know and was determined to find out. Two days later, I woke up and out of my mouth that I didn't seem to have control over at the time, I said, "His name is Nathaniel." This was the weirdest thing to me, as it felt like someone else had full control over my mouth - the Holy Spirit - and used it to deliver a message to me when I seemed to do a very good job at missing his initial introduction as I fell asleep. God is good and all you have to do is ask!

SCREAMS OF TORTURE

The next day, I was extremely excited to go to work. I couldn't wait to get there and experience the spiritual atmosphere with my eyes opening up. My curiosity for this new beginning was getting the best of me.

I stared into open space while getting ready for work, trying to see something while putting on my clothes at the same time. While driving to work, I kept myself aware of what was going on, but I didn't see anything out of the ordinary, though I wanted to. After arriving at work, I was a little scared because I knew that I was one of the only people that would be on my floor at 6:30 in the morning.

As I opened the door to the room of the cubicles for my team, I didn't notice anything out of the ordinary, so I just turned on the light and got to work. As time went by, more people started trickling in. Everything seemed normal for the first few hours, then out of nowhere I began to hear screams that were so loud that the entire floor should have been able to hear them. The screams were in a woman's voice and if I were to take a guess, it sounded like she was getting beaten or tortured. If I were to relate the sounds to anything, it would be sounds that you would hear from a horror movie.

I looked around in the room of cubicles that I was working in, everyone seemed normal and were on their computers as if nothing was going on. After hearing it a few more times, I leaned over and asked one of my cube mates if he heard anything. He looked at me as if I was crazy and asked, "Hear what, exactly?"

I knew at that moment that what I was hearing was in the spirit and that no one else could hear it, I responded with, "I hear what sounds like screams." He let me know that a few maintenance people were inspecting the bathroom and that some of the tools that they were using could be making the sound that I was hearing. Another guy in the cube interjected, "Sometimes the pipes in the restroom make a squealing sound when you turn on the water." I just nodded my head and came to the conclusion that I needed to rule both of these theories out.

I walked in the hallway to watch the maintenance people work. They were going into the restroom to take measurements for the revamping of the restroom and weren't using any tools that could possibly be making the sound that I was hearing. Next, my coworker went into the restroom to turn on the water, trying to get the pipes to make a sound. He came back and asked if I could hear it. I told him that I couldn't. At that point, I knew beyond the shadow of a doubt that my spiritual senses were opening up.

I WANT YOU TO SEE ME

In the cubicle room, I sat closest to the door and there were about 30 to 40 feet from our door to the stairwell exit door. A few hours after hearing the screams, at first in my peripherals and then in my natural sight I saw a black mass in front of the exit door that was getting bigger and smaller as if it were trying to get my attention. The mass didn't have a specific form, if I were to relate it to anything it would be a mix between the consistency of smoke, mist, and clouds but you couldn't see through it. It was blacker than black, pure darkness.

As I sat there staring at it, it didn't disappear like the two things that I had seen previously. It was as if this thing, which I thought to be a demon, wanted me to see it and knew that I had now been exercising my ability to see. After about 20 seconds of staring at this demon, it got smaller and finally disappeared. This was my first encounter seeing a demon in an open vision and though it was a little scary, I was happy to be able to see that it was there.

Two days later I gave my mother a call to let her know all of the things that were happening to me. I let her know about the demon that looked like a black mass and how it just stood there as if it wanted me to see it or wanted me to be intimidated.

To my surprise, she let me know that the day that I saw it, she had seen the same thing in front of her bedroom door that night. She stated that she had already turned out all of the lights and this thing was so black that it could be seen in what she thought to already be pitch black darkness. I took this as a threat and I wasn't going to stand for it. First, you come and you try to intimidate me and then when I didn't budge, you go to my mother. Second, I don't play when it comes to my family and I know who I can call on to get this taken care of.

In the snippets of Michael's books - that I hadn't bought yet - I read something about demons trying to scare people out of seeing in the spirit. It's one thing to believe that they exist because the Bible says so, but to see them face to face is an entirely different story. When one can see them or an angel, you don't just believe anymore, you know beyond the shadow of a doubt that everything in this Word is 100 percent true no matter what this world is trying to sway you toward.

I had believed the Word and now that the believing had turned into a knowing, I also knew that I could pray to have that demon taken out, stripped of his assignment, and have a hedge of protection surrounding my mother and I through warfare.

Some demons don't leave as easily as others do and some require prayer and fasting in order to get rid of. I wasn't going to take any chances and I pulled all of the stops. I planned a fast for my mother and I that weekend. It was the first fast that I had done without any food for three days. During this fast, I asked the Lord to send angels to sweep my mother's house clean and spiritually plead the blood of Jesus over every crack, crevice, wall, door, piece of carpet, and blade of grass on my mother's land. I was praying protection and heavenly atmosphere to invade the situation.

I didn't really know how to do spiritual warfare back then. All that I knew was that I wanted my mother protected.

At the end of the fast, I called my mother to see how she was doing. I never even mentioned that I was fasting for her and I. I wanted to know if she could tell a difference in her home without me telling her what I was doing.

She told me that she felt great and that she had a few updates for me. I was so excited to hear them that I sat at the edge of my seat. She told me that she was coming from the gym and as she was parking her car in the garage, she looked in the rearview mirror to see and angel from the side. The angel was darting past the garage area with its wings flared out and seemed to be going around the house in circles. I think that it may have been doing what I prayed for, and that was praying or ministering to the land that my mother's house sits on.

She also told me that there was one day that she was watching The Price Is Right while eating her breakfast, and in her peripheral vision, she saw a face peeking through the French doors in her living room, as if the angel thought to himself, "Let me just check on her and make sure that everything is alright." When she looked in the natural, she couldn't see anything. This particular angel has done this quite a few times after the fact as well, he loves to peek through the French doors while she's eating. The Lord swept her house clean and I was so excited to be a part of it.

CURIOSITY SCARED THE CAT

The experience with my mom, took me over the top. I was on an all time high and went ahead and ordered all of Michael's books at once. I got them the next day and immediately began reading them during my lunch breaks at work. One particular day, I was reading and a curious young new hire came over to me. He asked me what I was reading and I lifted up the book to show him the title. He said aloud, "Powerful Keys To Spiritual Sight" and proceeded to ask me if I really believe in all of that stuff. I told him that I didn't only believe it, but I had started seeing it for myself just a few days prior. He was immediately intrigued and hung on every word as I told him the story of the armored angel leg in my bedroom. By the end of our talk, he told me that he was going to get the books for himself so that he could begin his journey. I was excited for him and couldn't wait to hear back from him the following Monday, as it was a Friday.

I came into work and was ready to hear that he had taken a step toward the deeper things of the Lord. I usually got into work before most people even get out of bed to get ready, so the anticipation was getting to me.

He finally came in and I called him over to my cube, "Hey man, did you get a chance to check out the books?" I asked with a huge smile on my face. He responded with his body slightly shaking, "I don't want anything to do with that stuff, man." I looked at him, confused, "But just the other day you were so ready to get the books and see what the Lord opens up to you, what happened between now and then?"

It was hard for me to keep him still and from walking back to his desk. It seemed like just talking about it would require him to relive what seemed to be a traumatizing experience. He mustered up all of the courage he had, took a breath, and told me that when he got home that night he decided to open up his laptop to take a look at the books on Amazon.

He began getting tired and closed his laptop before ordering the books, then fell asleep. A few hours into sleeping he had a nightmare and jolted out of his sleep. When he opened his eyes, he saw a demon that had attached itself to the ceiling and was hanging down slightly above his face with red eyes. He said that he pulled the covers over his head and screamed, finally asking the Lord to "get this thing out of here!"

I listened to his story and the Holy Spirit let me know that the demon was trying to scare him out of seeing and had heard our previous conversation that Friday. The demon was on assignment to stop him before he even began.

MEETING MR. CLEAN & THE DIRT DEVIL

At this time period, I was excited that I was beginning to experience something new but I was beginning to get a little shaky about seeing in the spirit. I think that it was more so the fact that I couldn't control when I was able to see. Things were popping in and out of the atmosphere and it would startle me. I was always on alert and slightly anxious at times.

One particular day after working out, I went to my girlfriend's house to watch a movie. I didn't realize how exhausted I was from the workout and found myself nodding off in seconds of her leaving the room. She decided that she would go into the kitchen and as I sat on her sectional, I began to smell dirt in the air. I called out to her to see if she smelled anything out of the ordinary and she said that she didn't.

I knew at that moment that I was smelling something in the spirit, but whatever it was kept moving around and I could only smell the dirt when it got close enough.

I decided that I would kick my feet up on the sectional while she was in the kitchen. One of her dogs came over for some attention and I rubbed her head while lying there. After closing my eyes for what seemed like only 5 minutes or so, my body fell asleep and my spiritual eyes opened. I could see my girlfriend's dog still sitting there waiting for me to pet her again, but I also saw the culprit that carried around the scent of dirt.

There was another black dog in the spirit, and it was walking in circles around my girlfriend's dog. This dog was dirty and seemed to have what resembled dirt on its body. I jumped up and as I looked, I could only see my girlfriend's dog, though I was sure that dirty dog was still around somewhere.

That same night, as we were watching a movie we both ended up falling asleep. I was on one end of the sectional and she was on the other end. My body fell into a deep, comforting sleep and I began to hear myself slightly snoring.

As I lie there, my spiritual eyes opened again and I began observing the room. There was a very tall man dressed in all white garments standing in front of the television at first, and then he transitioned to sitting on the ottoman about two feet away from me. He had a bald head and was about 8 feet tall with a blue rope tied around his waist.

As we sat there looking at each other, it seemed like it suddenly dawned upon him that I could see him. He leaned forward slightly, squinted his eyes, and turned his head to the right the way a dog would if it heard a sound that it's not familiar with.

As soon as he did this I jumped because initially when he sat down he didn't move but by him turning his head like he was thinking to himself, "Can you see me?" was enough to startle me out of my body's sleep.

I have seen this angel a few times, though, I still don't know his name to this day. I call him Mr. Clean because he looks like Mr. Clean in the face. He tends to appear when I'm praying in the morning before I go to work.

I've caught him twice looking at me from my staircase and smiling as I passionately pray over my day and for the blessings of others.

THE PLANETARIUM

Even the angels were beginning to scare me. I had no gauge for some of the things that I was beginning to see. There was one particular day that I said the prayer in Michael's book again, the prayer that began it all. I had borrowed one of my girlfriend's dogs so that I wouldn't be alone for the night, I was officially ready for anything that I could possibly see in the spirit for that night. Everything seemed normal at first and I fell asleep as usual. Suddenly, about three hours into sleeping I rolled over and as I did so, the dog starts whining.

I open my eyes and all around me were balls of light, there had to be about 500 orbs all together.

Time seemed to stop as I looked. Some of them were on the walls, the ceiling, floating in mid-air, and even moving slowly.

Honestly, though I was awake - it felt like a dream and if I were to compare it to anything - it felt like I had all of my faculties in a dreamlike state. I am unsure as to whether I was out of my body at that specific moment or not.

LEARNING TRUE INTERCESSION

This isn't a testimony of seeing in the spirit, but it happened during the time of my eyes opening, so I decided to include it. One day I decided that I would go to Chili's and have a cheat meal. I ordered the food online and went to the to-go section of the restaurant to pick up the food that I had ordered. There was a young lady working there that took care of my order and charged my card. We began to converse as I'm always curious to know what a person's reason is for not experiencing joy and walking with their head up high. She told me that she was going through a custody battle with her ex-boyfriend concerning their child. She stated that he and his family wanted nothing to do with her and her child, but wanted custody of the child to be spiteful in some way. They also stated that she was unfit as a mother and she asked for me to pray for her. I grabbed my food and headed home.

As I was eating and talking to my girlfriend on the phone, I began to get an extreme headache and then my chest started to feel as if it were about to expand and burst open under the pressure. I got off the phone with my girlfriend and all of my thoughts seemed to be directed toward the girl at Chili's. The Lord told me to pray and I took off in prayer. It seemed like the more I began to pray the more tears began to run down my face. During prayer, the Lord told me that he was allowing me to feel what she feels in order to be able to pray the way that He would like me to. I had never experienced anything like that before in my life.

It was no longer about just writing someone's name on a sheet of paper to be reminded to pray for them, and when you do pray, the prayer is quick and simple, "Lord, please help this person. Amen." and then move on to the next person on the list.

No, the Lord was teaching me that you pray as if you were in that situation, you pray as if your life is on the line, you pray as if you are praying for your own children or mother or wife, etc. I began to get extremely hot, so much so that it felt like fire was pulsating through my veins and off of my body.

The fire that I had felt two days prior had returned and after about 30 minutes or so, my headache and chest pain disappeared.

I reached out to her the next day because I wanted to confirm what the Lord was teaching me. I sent her a message on Facebook Messenger to find out what happens to her when she is under a lot of stress. She told me that she gets extreme chest pains and headaches and this is exactly what I was feeling as I was praying for her. The Lord is amazing!

Two days prior to this testimony, I had written down people's names on a sheet of paper so that I could go down the list every night to pray for them. The prayers that I was praying were relatively simple in stature and had no passion behind them. I was just praying as I had always known to pray because growing up in a Baptist church you don't learn these things, it was more so about head knowledge and preaching, not actual doing and experience. If things were being experienced, it was not being shared with the congregation so that they know what to expect and how to act accordingly. As I was going down the list of people to pray for, the Lord spoke to me and said, "Pray in tongues."

I responded out loud and said, "Lord, I don't know how to do that." I didn't hear anything for a few minutes. It was almost as if He was using the silence to help me to make a decision whether to be obedient or just sit there. Him not saying anything further spoke to me as if to say, "I've told you what to do, please do it." So, I lifted up my left hand, opened my mouth, and began to speak.

As soon as I began to speak, I felt fire that came from the tip of my left middle finger down to my elbow and extended to the rest of my body. I felt like I was on fire with the accompaniment of goosebumps from head to toe. This was me being baptized in the Holy Spirit, being baptized by fire.

HEATWAVE ANGELS

In Michael's book, *Supernatural Transportation*, I had been reading about traveling in the spirit like John in Revelation chapter 4. Two days after my eyes were opened, I decided that I would try to travel in the spirit. Every other Friday I was off from work, so I thought that it would be a perfect opportunity to stay up late and wait until something happened.

As soon as I got off work, I went upstairs and got into a rested position on my bed and began to focus with my eyes closed. It was particularly difficult to keep my eyes closed without the intention of falling asleep. I was there for about 45 minutes before slightly moving my body and opening my eyes. When I opened them I saw the most peculiar thing, I saw what looked like clear rectangular shapes around me. If I were to describe them in more detail - if you have ever seen Xmen when Xavier goes into Cerebro to find a specific mutant - the spiritual bricks looked like the walls of Cerebro. I'm not sure if these were scales or not, but the longer I lay there with my eyes open, the more they faded away until I couldn't see them anymore.

Later that night, I stayed up late mostly because I was scared to close my eyes and then wake up to find something staring back at me. When 2 a.m. rolled around, I decided that I would try to travel again. I closed my eyes and began to wait on the Lord. Once again,

I didn't experience anything and at this time it was about 3:30 a.m. before I opened my eyes again.

When I opened my eyes and sat up on the bed there were figures that I was seeing that were walking through my house. The figures looked like they could be people or at least the outline of a person, but instead of having skin on their bodies there was only the outline with a heatwave consistency on the inside.

While I sat there, I started to notice that there was more than just two or three of them, and I began to be able to distinguish between them as they paced the office area outside of my bedroom and also my bathroom. I was instantly reminded of how I said the prayer, welcoming them into my home every morning. Then I thought to myself that these must be members of the angelic armies and other heavenly beings that are in the prayer from Michael's book. I asked them to minister to my home in the prayer and it looked like they were pacing the floor and praying over different areas and sections of my house, as if each being had a specific area that it was assigned to pray over and they were doing it over and over again.

I didn't speak at this time and sat there for about 15 to 20 minutes before things began to fade away, though, I'm sure that they were still there. Make no mistake about it, when we pray things happen whether you can see it while it is happening or not.

HOW DO YOU USE THIS MACHINE?

There are only four places that I frequent on a consistent basis, that is Walmart, the gym, my job and of course my townhouse. One particular day, I was at the gym and there was a guy that the Lord had been directing me to. He was a lifter that had been considering doing a bodybuilding show. Initially, I didn't know much about him, only that the Lord wanted to be in his life and that He wanted to use me to lead him in a prayer to receive Jesus as his Lord and Savior.

I knew that the Lord likes to use my personality in people's lives to build rapport and minister to them, so I began to do just that. Over the miracle of time I learned a little bit about him and his family. He was married, had four kids at the time, and went through bouts of depression when he was off of his steroid cycles.

The bouts with depression allowed him the excuse to be able to justify the fact that he had a wife at home and also a girlfriend in the gym that he would openly and intimately kiss while people were working out. He was openly cheating on his wife and had no qualms admitting it. His girlfriend knew that he had a wife and kids, but neither of them cared about the situation. He and his girlfriend were both in the dark place of depression and were alright as long as they weren't alone in that place. Misery loves company, but I was determined to be used to allow the light in, so that neither of them would be the company that misery likes to keep.

I didn't work out with him very often, but when I did, I always found a way to bring the Lord into the conversations that we would have during our rests between sets. He seemed more concerned in trying to correct me in head knowledge that I could tell he gained from reading articles online or listening to people - who were atheists - that shared the same view of Christianity he did.

If I were to ask questions, he was very good at diverting the question to something he had researched in the atheist community to throw me off from where the Lord wanted to take the conversation. The Lord told me to keep coming, so that's exactly what I did. I just had my work cut out for me.

After a few months of him dating the girl from the gym, word began to get around about how him and his girlfriend's mother - who also works out at the gym - took it upon herself to start arguments in the gym and put his personal business out there for everyone in the gym to hear. She was concerned for her daughter and who she was seeing and didn't want to see her get hurt because he had a wife. The boyfriend girlfriend side relationship was falling apart and I began to see less of him at the gym.

One day I messaged him on Facebook Messenger to see if we could meet up, talk about the Lord, and just connect. He said that he was willing and actually wanted to talk with me about getting saved. I was surprised and thought to myself how much power there is in brokenness. He worked weird hours and got off at night, and because of this he asked me to meet him at the gym to talk at midnight. I thought the request was kind of weird, but this was another chance to be used and I wasn't going to miss out on it! I was off the next day, so losing a little bit of sleep didn't mean very much to me. I cared a lot about him getting saved and knowing beyond the shadow of a doubt that he would have eternal life. I accepted his request and decided that I would meet him at the gym.

Because I was seeing so much at this time, I always had my girlfriend's dog with me to keep me company as seeing in the spirit isn't so scary when you are experiencing it with someone else or a pet. We made it to the gym at 11:50 and I brought the dog inside. There were only three people there as I walked around the gym to find him. There was a couple walking on the treadmill together, and a man in the back room lifting free weights. I decided that I would sit in the front and just wait for him. I messaged him and didn't get an answer and decided that I would stay until 12:30 just to be sure that I didn't miss him.

The couple that was walking on the treadmill got off, petted the dog and left. As I sat there looking down at my phone, out of nowhere the dog began to growl and bark, showing her teeth as if she was ready to attack. I had never seen her like this and it immediately startled me. As I looked up to see what had gotten her so worked up, I noticed a college kid standing in front of me. I had previously seen him around at the gym and had shared a few conversations with him. For the sake of his anonymity, we will call him Josh.

I paused as I watched him staring emotionlessly at the snarling dog that was pulling on the leash. He didn't seem to be himself, as anyone in their right mind wouldn't stand two feet from a dog that was ready to attack. Josh looked up at me, smiled and asked, "What are you doing here so late?" Knowing that I was sitting in the front and everyone who came in had to pass me, and knowing that I had already walked around the entire gym, even the restrooms and Josh was nowhere to be found, I asked "Where did you come from? You weren't here when I got here and your car isn't outside." I looked outside again to make sure that what I was saying was true.

He completely deflected my question and set his gaze on the piece of equipment that he was standing closest to, the stair master. He smirked with darkness in his eyes and asked, "How do you use this machine?" I paused and stared at him for a minute, looking into his eyes trying to find some type of sign that would tell me that he was still human. His whole countenance had changed from the Josh that I knew from all of the times that I had previously seen him at the gym. There was a darkness about him and I began to think that he was possessed. I told the dog to lie down and I got up to show him how to use the machine. I walked over to the machine and started, "All you have to do is step on the machine, select the…"

I turned to my side and noticed that as soon as I began talking his head dropped lifelessly and he leaned over slightly, his hands dangled from his body as if he no longer had control of them, and his body began to rock forwards and backwards. At this point I knew that there was something demonic going on here. This was like a movie scene. I stood there looking for about 30 seconds until he snapped out of it.

Once he snapped out of it, he proceeded to ask me the same question again, "How do you use this machine?" It was almost as if there was a shifting between him and the demons that were working through him and when the demons took control, he lost control of all of his faculties. I paused and looked at him for a minute and began showing him how to use the machine again and the same slow rocking process happened again.

This happened a third time with him asking me the same question and me trying to show him until finally, I told him to have a good night and left. I didn't feel like I knew spiritual warfare at the time and was afraid to lay hands on him to pray, so I just left. All of these spiritual experiences were new to me and I wasn't confident in moving out of them yet, spiritual warfare and deliverance being one of them. As I was leaving, I thought to myself how someone could appear out of thin air and later read that people dealing with the occult and demons often travel through the spirit by demonic means.

The following Monday I came to the gym and spoke with Josh, all of his faculties seemed to be in check and he seemed like a regular person. I talked with him about what happened and he told me that he wrestled with Schizophrenic and that demons tell him things, tempt him to kill himself, and take him places.

They also choke him, scratch him, drag him, and lift his bed off the floor at night. I proceeded to talk with him about Jesus and how if he received Him that all of the demonic activity in his life would stop through prayer. He told me that he was actually liking them in his life at that point. He told me that Jesus was just a man, and that God did not come in the flesh when I asked him to be sure.

```
This is how you can recognize the
Spirit of God: Every spirit that
acknowledges that Jesus Christ
has come in the flesh is from God,
but every spirit that does not
acknowledge Jesus is not from God.
(1 John 4:2-3 NIV)
```

Josh was fascinated by the things of the spirit, just like I was. The only difference was that he was being introduced to the dark side of things. There was a complete duality between experiencing the joy of the Lord and His kingdom versus the enemy striking fear into a person and showing a false reality of something "good".

He stated many times how powerful it made him feel to be able to experience some of the things that demons were showing him. After many months and talks with Josh - him sharing what the demons were doing for him, me ministering the Gospel to him, and many bouts of prayer on my end behind the scenes - he came up to me and let me know that he was ready to be saved one day at the gym. He stated that he was ready to know Jesus, as all of his friends were Christians and were taking him to church. They had been used to also minister to him.

We then proceeded to go through a prayer of salvation and in the coming days - even to the time of writing this book - Josh has not experienced anymore demonic activity in his life. In addition, he no longer has to take the medication for schizophrenia. He is free!

Concerning the other lifter, he apologized for not messaging me and not showing up. He asked me to help him receive Jesus because he didn't know how. I led him through a prayer of salvation and also let him know that it is not only important to just say the words, repeating after me, but to mean them in his heart and with all of his being. He did this and it has been a rocky journey of growth for him. Things soon ended with his side girlfriend and he began to get help for his addiction to steroids and mended things back together with his wife and family.

He moved out to Colorado and started a training business for fitness athletes. I've seen him grow and the Lord work in his life in terms of ridding him of all of the unnecessary garbage that we are so good at accumulating without the Lord's influence in our lives.

He brings us from glory to glory (2 Cor. 3:18) while also shedding light on the things and areas that are necessary for our growth.

THE CORPORATE PROFESSIONAL

This particular day, I woke up excited to see what the Lord was going to show me. With my eyes now open I often wavered between being scared and so curious to see what the Lord was saying or trying to teach me that I was willing to sacrifice the fear in order to just see and learn. I wanted the full experience and knew that meant seeing demons as well. It's not practical to believe that when your eyes are open that you will only see things of heaven and its goodness. I wanted to also be able to see the strategies of darkness so that I could be used as a beacon of light to be able to fight against them.

I went to work and constantly asked the Lord to show me something. I didn't see anything all day until it was time for lunch. I usually packed all of my food and headed over to the break area, which had a microwave.

On my floor of the building, the break area is actually in the middle of a hallway, so people walk past it to get to their seats even if they don't have to use it. It is not the best area to wait and heat up your food because there is so much traffic with people walking past and on top of that, there is nowhere to sit and enjoy your meal.

As I stood there watching the microwave countdown with my food inside, I saw someone coming down the hall in my right side peripherals. I didn't feel the need to turn as the person was coming toward me because they were so far away, probably about 30 feet, and it's a normal thing to see people walking toward you in this high traffic area. As the person got closer, I began to notice something strange about them, they were dressed in all black, so I thought.

Then when they got about 5 feet away from me, I realized that the person wasn't just dressed in all black, they were all black, they looked like a shadow, yet I could see straight through them. In an instant, when I realized this I began to turn my head to see them better and as soon as I did it was like they knew that I was turning to see them, so they turned down a path between the cubicles right before reaching me. I bolted after them because I knew that this was something spiritual and I didn't want to miss it, demon or not.

I turned the corner only to find that there was no one there, which was strange because any real person wouldn't have been able to get away from me that quickly especially considering they were only 5 feet away from me at that point in time.

It is documented that some people have seen these shadows standing in corners of their room or on the side of their bed, watching them as they fall asleep. They call them "shadow people", but I only have one name for them, demons.

STRIKING GOLD IN THE MIDDLE OF ATLANTA

I'm a Georgia boy, I was born in Decatur, grew up in the Snellville area, and graduated from Georgia Tech. So, when there was a training opportunity there for my job in Cyber Security at the time, naturally I hopped on the opportunity to go back to my stomping grounds and roots. It was great because I would be able to see my family and get the training that I needed for my job at the same time.

I got to the hotel and one of the first things that I did was pray over my room and the entire building because I didn't know what took place on the land the hotel was built on and I didn't know what took place in the room that was assigned to me. I wanted to make sure that the building was conducive for the atmosphere of heaven to penetrate it. I prayed and pleaded the blood of Jesus over the building and asked for the angels to manifest themselves and minister to the land, the building, the rooms, and all of the people. I asked the Lord to stir up a fire and a burning desire in all of the people, believer or not, to want to get to know Him and to develop a deeper relationship with Him.

On the morning of the first training session, I wanted to see if I could pray for hours on end. I had read about Michael praying for hours and I wanted to try it for myself. I knew that it was possible to pray in english for long periods of time, but that would mean that I would actually have to think about it, which could take away from the lesson. So, I decided to pray in tongues for the entirety of the ten hour class. The interesting thing about praying in tongues is that once you begin, you'll have to think about it in order to continue doing it. But if you keep going for about 15 minutes, it's like your spirit fully takes over and your mouth just keeps moving on its own without any mental processes taking place concerning prayer. You are free to do other things while still in prayer.

After the class, I noticed that I was still in prayer, so I just kept going until it was time to go to sleep. But even while I slept, my mind kept praying which was very interesting to me. I had never experienced anything like this before and it now makes perfect sense concerning what the Lord means when He tells us to pray without ceasing (1 Thes 5:16-18). It is definitely possible, and I think that He means it literally, not figuratively.

When I woke up I began to pray under my breath again and throughout another class. During a break, I went back to my room and noticed that the cleaning person had not come in yet. Then I noticed that there was gold glitter all over my bed, all over the bag I packed, on my clothes inside the bag, and on the floor around the bag. Initially, I thought that one of the cleaning people came into my room and did this. I remember thinking to myself, "How dare they come into my room and sprinkle glitter all over my stuff! Do they know how hard it is to get glitter out of anything?!"

I tried shaking it out of my clothes and wiping it off of my bed to no avail. I laugh about my reaction now after knowing what it was. The gold dust actually has a consistency that is finer than any glitter and it would be extremely difficult to pick up just one piece of it or shake it off of anything.

I left the room and came back later after the final session of the training and all of the gold dust was gone completely. There wasn't even a trace of it in or on the carpet anymore. With this said, anyone who has ever done anything with arts and crafts and has used glitter as a tool in art knows that it is almost impossible to get glitter out of anything. Even after vacuuming, you will still find traces of glitter on whatever material it has been on, especially the carpet. I sat down for a second, and the Holy Spirit said, "That was gold dust, son." I had a huge laugh after this just thinking about how I reacted to my first experience with gold dust. Thanks, Lord!

CALL TO ACTION

Think about when you were younger, when you went to a school dance, or when you got a new toy for Christmas, or one of the best memories that you have. One thing that you will realize while thinking of those memories is that your senses are immediately engaged. Some of us can even remember the smell of someone's perfume or cologne just by recalling a memory. When we read our Bible, this childlike imagination and activation of our senses is what we should embrace if we desire to see.

This imagination coupled with a relationship to God and an obedient lifestyle WILL open your eyes. Begin to read the Bible and embrace it literally as the Lord leads you and embrace everything as if you are there. I pray that the Lord opens your eyes so that you may see.

CHAPTER 6
BEING HELD BACK

In the midst of all of the excitement with everything that the Lord was showing me, I was struggling in my relationship with my girlfriend. The constant back and forth between her and I was at a complete max. Not only did I feel like I had to choose between her and the Lord, but she began to say that I was crazy because of the things that I was seeing on a consistent basis. In addition, now that I had been set free from perversion, I didn't view women the same way anymore - thinking of them as objects - and in turn, didn't want to have sex with her anymore unless we were married. She began making comments like, "Maybe it's because we don't have sex anymore that all of these problems are starting in our relationship." In that moment, I thought to myself that she probably needed deliverance and an intervention of the Lord's power.

ROOTED IN JEALOUSY

I wanted her to begin to experience some of the things that I was experiencing with the Lord. She was a Christian, but only in the sense of wearing an invisible name tag that said "Christian", not really willing to take steps of faith to actually see God work - sadly, this is the state of the majority of the church. I asked her if she felt comfortable with us praying over her house together, welcoming the Lord in and using the house as a beacon for His manifest presence. She agreed to it and we both went to her house after the gym. We didn't have any oil, so we prayed over water instead.

As we began praying over the house, which was mostly me praying, she began to act like she didn't necessarily want to be there. She began to complain about us not using oil and using water instead, and when it came time for us to pray over the land she proceeded to argue with me saying, "This seems like a ritual, and what is the point of actually walking around the house? Can't we just pray from inside and it have the same affect?" I told her, "Look, if you don't want to do it, go inside and I'll do it. It's important that we walk the land and our feet touch it. The Lord told Joshua that every place that the sole of his foot shall tread upon, that has He given unto him, as He said unto Moses (Josh 1:3). We are claiming this promise over your land and your household and putting the forces of darkness on notice that we know it." She ended up joining me in walking around her house, but she did so reluctantly.

I began to tell people about my spiritual journeys with the Lord as I worked out with her in the gym. The people as well as myself were excited to hear my stories as I seemed to always have a new one day after day. People would request to hear about what the Lord was doing in my life in hopes that they would eventually experience the same thing in their life. Sometimes in the middle of me telling a story of what the Lord had shown me, she would interject and make a comment that would make the story seem like it was of lesser importance than it was.

I remember talking with her about this one day and she got a little flustered in her response stating, "I said the exact same prayer that you said, but I'm not experiencing any of the things that you are. It just feels like you're a part of some little secret club with God and I have no place there and honestly, I can't relate." I realized at that moment that all of the acting out that she was doing was rooted in jealousy and that she actually wanted the experiences that I was having. I found out that she had always wanted experiences like this in her life, and now that someone close to her was having them on a regular basis, it made her angry that she wasn't experiencing them too. Honestly, there was nothing that I could do at this point other than pray, that was between her and the Lord and I wasn't going to intervene.

SHE'S NOT YOUR WIFE

Dear reader, if you have made it this far in the book, my intent is not to bash my ex-girlfriend. I did things wrong in the relationship as well. The Lord is having me share the struggle in the relationship as there are people that will read this book that have been praying for confirmation to move forward in marriage and are facing a similar struggle. That struggle is being in a relationship with someone that does not share your passion for Christ and is not willing to either.

We were arguing so much - even more so now that I was experiencing more of God - that I began to think to myself that she may not be "the one" for me. Even though we were going through our issues and arguing, breaking up with her and getting back together with her out of guilt, and her struggling with her belief in the Lord - I still wanted to marry her at some point down the line. I had grown up in an environment with a lot of arguing, but I was determined to make things work in my relationship, knowing that we both loved each other.

One day after arguing, I decided to take the day off from the gym and just consult the Lord more fervently in the situation to see what He thought. I had listened to a sermon on inviting the Lord into everything that you do and I decided that I would do just that in our relationship. As soon as I got home, I stood in the living room, lifted my hands, and was about to pray, "Lord, please let your kingdom come into our relationship." The Lord interrupted me in the middle of the prayer and said bluntly, "She is not your wife."

The effect of His words were so powerful that they stopped me from moving my mouth. I tried praying the same prayer again and the Lord invaded my thoughts once again and told me that she wasn't my wife. Though I knew that I was hearing the Lord correctly, I wanted confirmation. I wanted Him to speak to me in the way that I had always known Him to do so, through another person. I told her about everything that was going on and we both decided to wait for more confirmation.

IF SHE WERE TO NEVER CHANGE

At this point, the relationship was starting to take a toll on me. It was very draining to try to keep my focus on the Lord and uphold the relationship with her, but I was still trying to hang in there. I was so passionate about the Lord that I began pushing her to read certain books, look at certain YouTube videos, and consult certain people. It was wrong of me to do this as it pushed her to a place that she just didn't want to be. I wanted her to have a passion for the Lord like I did, but I didn't realize that this was something that couldn't be forced into a person.

If the person isn't ready or if they don't have the passion to pursue God on their own then there is nothing that anyone in this world can do to force them. They have to come to that place on their own with the Lord.

I had been talking with a strong Christian that worked as a marriage counselor at one point in his life. He preaches at Transformation Church in Tulsa from time to time and he was working at my corporate job as well. I spoke to him about what was going on in my life, not knowing that he had been a marriage counselor in the past. Immediately after telling him the situation, he smiled and began to speak. He said, "I've seen this a lot in marriage counseling in the past.

There is always one person in the relationship that is on fire for the Lord and the other person just seems to be getting dragged along reluctantly, holding the passionate person back. The passionate person desires for the reluctant person to be brought up to speed, so that they can go ahead and get married and build the reluctant person up so that they can both share the same passion and grow together with the Lord. Do you feel like you're being held back?" I was already nodding my head and replied, "Yes." He continued, "Then I will bring something to your attention. This girl was like this in the beginning when you first met her. You could have called it off then, but you didn't because you wanted to help her grow. She began to grow to a certain extent, but once she felt like you were too far gone and it required for her to have to face things that she wasn't willing to face, her progress stopped and you became pushy trying to force growth."

This guy was hitting the nail on the head with everything that he was saying, in fact, when I would bring those types of things up in conversation with her, it would always start an argument.

He went further, "Let me ask you something, if she were to stay the same person that she is right now for the rest of her life, would you be willing to stay with her? If the answer is no, then you have some serious thinking to do." After he said this, he got up from the table and left. After he left, I thought about what he said and my answer was no. I also knew that the Lord was using him to bring me the confirmation that I was looking for. I was happy, but also sad because I had invested so much time in her and I was emotionally attached.

LETTING IT ALL GO

Because I was so passionate about the Lord and forceful in my approach to leading her in a direction that she just wasn't ready to go, she called a break in the relationship. She wanted time to think things through, and honestly, I knew what I needed to do but I wasn't willing to do it. I needed to drop the relationship all together as the Lord had been revealing to me, but it was just tough. I had invested so much time into one person and I felt like I was the one responsible for a lot of her growth. She had no one but me around to invest in her spiritual development.

After the break was over, we decided to have a movie night with food and fun. When I got to her house, she was in the kitchen cooking a few things. I gave her a kiss and proceeded to walk back to the living room to sit on the sofa. The Lord spoke to me in that moment and asked, "Why are you entertaining this?" I looked down, knowing what must be done. When she came into the living room ready to watch the movie, she asked me if I wanted a massage.

She knew that I liked massages and I guess this was her attempt at trying to show me that she appreciated me. I turned it down and a few minutes later told her that the relationship wasn't going to work. As soon as I said this, her eyes filled up with tears and she went into the kitchen to grab a plastic bag. She began filling the bag up with all of my belongings, things that I had left over her house. I grabbed the bag and left right away. I was so grateful to God for intervening and reminding me of what needed to be done.

EYES CLOSED

During my struggles with the relationship, I was seeing so much in the spirit that it began to scare me. Things were popping in and out of sight on such a consistent basis that it was causing me to be on alert everywhere that I turned. My heart would race at times, trying to make it through the day, but at the same time I would consistently ask the Lord to show me things. It sounds almost idiotic that I would ask and then when I saw something, I would jump, but the truth is, I wanted these things to be so normal in my life that I wouldn't become scared anymore. All of the jumpiness and anxiety of seeing, though I wanted it, began to get the best of me and I made one of the biggest mistakes of my life. I asked the Lord to slow things down with my spiritual sight and bring it back to me in its full expression later, when "I'm ready."

Dear reader, I urge you to never ask the Lord to slow things down if He has opened your spiritual eyes and is moving you toward a deeper spiritual relationship with Him. Instead, ask Him to give you grace to walk better in both realms and to not be fearful of what you may see. Ask Him to instruct and teach you in the way you should go, to counsel you with His eye upon you (Psalms 32:8). At the time of writing this, it has been over two years since I have seen strong, full figured, open visions on a consistent basis like I did before asking that of the Lord.

I still see, but only small things like orbs and flashes of light, and colors around people in my minds eye, but not how I did before.

I will tell you that once you experience the things of heaven - angels, scents, voices, Jesus, etc. - anything that you see on this earth just becomes dull. Not even the greatest pictures and most colorful sunrises or sunsets amount to the brilliance of colors and landscapes that He can and will show you. Nothing amounts to it. Thankfully, the Lord has told me that I am now ready, and I feel it, the only thing is that I'll have to practice waiting on Him whereas before all I had to do was say a simple prayer out of a book.

WHAT'S LOVE GOT TO DO WITH IT?

As my eyes began to close more and more over time, it was as if my desire to see began to grow. Strong spiritual sight had become a part of my life for the six months or so that I was seeing on a regular basis. Now that my eyes were closing, I didn't necessarily know what to do with myself. There was no more adventure to life anymore and everything just seemed dull, going through the monotonous motions of work, the gym, and back home. Though I was partly scared of having my spiritual sight, at least I could expect an adventure every time I started the day, everyday. Even if I hadn't seen anything for the day, I could expect something amazing when I got home in the form of a dream or electric force fields in door entrances or heavenly scents ranging from frankincense to flowers. I never knew what to expect or what the Lord was going to show me next and that brought excitement to my life.

After a few months of not experiencing anything other than small orbs of lights flashing in and out of the atmosphere, I began to get angry with the Lord. Like, how dare He take away something that I asked Him to take away? Out of my anger I went into a little rebellious phase and without realizing it at the time, began to move out of a religious mindset and the mindset of a slave. A slave thinks to himself or herself, "If I do enough for my master, then my master will..." I began to do everything with the sole purpose of my spiritual eyes opening again.

Instead of praying for healing over people at Walmart because I loved them, I was praying in obedience but with ulterior motives of receiving something in return. I was seeing the Lord heal people right before my eyes, but I couldn't seem to shake the "if I scratch your back, you scratch mine" mentality.

I then began to beat people over the head with the Word to show how much I knew intellectually about Him. The Word is 100 percent true when it says that knowledge puffs up while love builds up (1 Cor. 8:1). I was only puffing myself up with the way that I was using my knowledge of the Word, and sadly this is how some of the Word is being preached in churches around the world - minus the beating over the head. Instead of Christian leaders preaching in a way that leads people to God, they are preaching in a way that leads people to them.

People end up talking about the pastor, rather than being led to the source, Christ. During this time period I wanted the glory versus humbling myself and letting people know where the knowledge, wisdom, and understanding came from. God is the source of ALL things whether we want to believe it or not, and we should be giving Him the glory no matter what.

In my personal opinion, the Word does not mean anything in

the heart of a believer until the believer loves Jesus Christ. Before this point, the Bible just seemed like a book filled with rules of things that people should and should not do to have a better life on earth before passing away and an eternal life after. When someone loves someone else - a spouse, a girlfriend, a boyfriend - they will go to great lengths to take care of that person and nurture the relationship out of that love, without any selfish ulterior motives in mind.

Because I was beginning to go back to living by a standard of rules, rather than that of a functioning relationship with God and grace, everything was centered around me doing something so that He would open the door spiritually for me. I began to strictly listen to gospel music, only watch movies that were Biblical, and only read books that had something to do with God. Though, I do believe that it is important to be good shepherds of all of our senses and everything that we do for the glory of God (1 Cor. 10:31), it is important to know where that passion is coming from and where it is rooted. The passion should come from a place of deep love for the Lord and desire to want to strengthen the relationship that one has already started with Him, not from a place of doing something to get something out of the Lord. He knows what we are doing and knew about it before it even became a thought for us. I thought that I was moving closer to God by doing these things, but because my root was founded in myself and not Christ, I got burnt out relatively quickly - after about a year or so.

CALL TO ACTION

There are some people in our lives and relationships that we deeply love, but we know that the longer that we keep them in our lives, the more it hinders our relationship with God. It is really tough, because we have invested so much time and effort into our relationship with this person. If this is you and you desire to know what the Lord thinks about the situation, say the below prayer.

"Lord, I don't know what to do in this situation. It is like the closer I get to this person, the further I get from You. Lord, I ask that You help me to bring things to an end if this relationship is not of You and Your will for my life and give me plain confirmation before doing so. Amen."

CHAPTER 7

GREAT LESSONS LEARNED

After my relationship with my ex girlfriend, I found myself in a state of loneliness, even though I didn't recognize it at first. I wasn't allowing myself time to actually sit down and sort through my emotions. I was in a consistent mindset of moving forward and continual growth. This mindset came out in the gym and my workplace, pushing my limits to no end.

Slowly but surely, I began to read the Word less and my prayer life wasn't as powerful as it normally was. Because I wasn't allowing myself time to sort through my emotions with the Lord and grow, I found myself doing things that were geared toward my own personal success and not necessarily what my Father was doing in heaven. My focus had shifted from the Lord to myself and because it happened gradually over time, I didn't recognize it at first.

Before I knew it, I wasn't spending time with the Lord anymore and began to look at women differently, slowly I began to objectify them in my mind as I once did when I was wholeheartedly living in the world. For some reason, I saw myself falling but I was too burnt out to pick up the slack.

As I continued to grow stagnant in my walk with Jesus, I began to compromise my standards. I felt myself begin to entertain a willingness to pick up my old lifestyle and fell into temptation. I felt so bad about everything afterwards that I immediately turned to the Lord the next day. I was beginning to feel empty on the inside and I desired my relationship with Him. I needed it and it couldn't wait any longer.

During work the next day, I was looking up proper ways to do a consecration fast - a fast that a person goes on for the sole purpose of being cleansed. I knew that something was completely off with me and I wanted to humble myself before the Lord. As I was leaving my job, I couldn't help but break out in tears. It was a Thursday and I had already eaten that day, but I wanted to start my fast immediately so that I wouldn't have the chance to talk myself out of it. Once I got home I took a nap, shortly after I woke up and spent some time in prayer. I asked the Lord to honor the fast that I was about to do and began reading my Bible. I asked Him again to honor the fast because I didn't hear anything from Him. When I turned my head back to my Bible, I heard the Lord say, "Go eat." I thought that it was an interesting request because He knew that I was trying to fast and get into a place where it would just be Him and I.

So, thinking that I may have heard Him wrong, I got more proactive in my approach and stood up in the living room with my hands raised as I prayed. I asked Him to honor it again and He said the same thing with more urgency, "Go eat!" I stood there for a second and decided to ask for confirmation, "Lord, this is a strange request as I'd like to start my fast. If this is You, please give me confirmation." Right after asking this, lightning struck my house. It was pretty comical as I stood there wondering if that was the confirmation that I should be looking for.

So I asked, "Lord, if that was You I ask that you do it again." Right then in that moment, lightning struck my house again! I grabbed my keys and started toward the garage, opened the garage door and then thought to myself that because a storm was brewing that could be the cause of the lightning. I had never known the Lord to confirm with lightning before, so I came back into the house. I sat there for a second, thinking, and then decided to ask Him to confirm it again, "Lord, if…." Before I could even ask for confirmation, lightning struck my house again, but this time it was accompanied by stronger thunder than before. The thunder literally shook my whole house and I looked up with a smile and said, "Okay. I'm going to eat!"

PROVOKER OF ALL CHANGE

The next day, when I woke up for the start of the fast I felt completely refreshed and ready for the day. I wasn't sure why the Lord didn't want me to begin the night before, but none of that mattered. All that mattered was that I was moving out of obedience, I didn't need to know the "why" component of what He was telling me to do, only that He told me to do it and I did. I was excited to go along with it and I asked the Lord to reveal to me everything that I needed to repent for, along with teaching me lessons along the way.

As I read the Word, the Lord began to speak to me and tell me things about myself, things that brought me to tears and in some cases broke me down to my knees. He started off by saying, "I am the provoker of all change (Dan 2:20-21)!" When He said this to me, I began to become a little afraid because of the tone that He took with me. It was extremely intense, but I needed to know what else He had to say. He continued, "When you were in a relationship with your ex girlfriend, you began to think to yourself that you were causing all of the change in her life. In reality it was Me through you that was bringing the change.

I was the one that was conditioning her heart, I was the one watering the seed, I was the one that was bringing people in her life to influence her decisions, not you! It is prideful for you to think that you can change someone. If you had allowed Me into the situation, you would have been drawing from an everlasting source which takes the weight off of yourself. You would tell people to thank Me when I was using you to deliver messages to them, but in your heart you wanted the recognition. If they didn't acknowledge you, then you would allow it to have an affect on you - this is false humility. You wanted people to come to you in order to get to Me, rather than just teaching them to come to me directly. You have no power to change anyone outside of Me." As He was speaking, I ended up on my knees asking Him to forgive me. Tears were running down my face as I was being taught this lesson. I never expected to be scolded for what I was doing because I thought that I was doing things right.

As I was on the floor, He continued speaking in a less intense voice, "When you begin to try to take things into your own hands, you try to move the person at your pace. She wasn't ready to move as fast as you. You became frustrated with her because you didn't want to marry her if you two weren't in the same place with Me. You felt like you were being dragged down and she felt like she was being forced to move forward in order to keep you in her life." All of these things were coming at me both in my mind's eye and through invasions of my thoughts.

The replaying of some of the events that took place between her and I in my mind were so powerful. He was showing me specific instances in our relationship that I would become frustrated, impatient, and intense to get my point across to her. I couldn't do anything else but cry. I felt like I was already broken from the relationship, but at this point of Him reproving me, I felt like I was falling lower than low. He was breaking me down to my core, to my bare minimums and I was thankful that He was. I wanted to learn everything that He had to teach me, no matter how much it hurt - I wanted to grow.

The images in my mind began to slow down after a few hours and I began reading *A Loving Life* by Paul Miller. It is a great book concerning the love of God displayed through the Bible and how we can take practical steps to display that love. I learned relatively quickly that love is not a feeling, no matter how much Disney and Hollywood would like to portray it as such. Then the Lord spoke to me again through both the writings of the book and even after I put it down.

I didn't realize that I was being led to read certain books at the time of my fast, I thought I was just picking them up on my own accord. He said to me, "People's feelings change all the time. Some people even base their entire life - making every decision - on how they feel about the specific topic at hand. They follow what they see on television and this is an inaccurate display of love. People move in and out of relationships because the person that they once had feelings for doesn't make them feel the way that they once did in the beginning of the relationship. They divorce and have affairs because the person that they are with no longer makes them feel what they once felt. This is what they are being shown on television and the state of the world is following it. Satan wants people to believe that their love for someone is rooted in their feelings because once he can get people to believe that, then they will never be able to stay in committed relationships with others - whether that is a friendship, boyfriend and girlfriend, or marriage.

They will always bounce around, because their feelings will sway at every bend in the wind." I was so blown away at the things that He was telling me. I was reminded of how Frank would always tell me that television is called television for a reason, it tells you a vision. He would say, "That little box that we are so enthused to get home to after work is teaching us things every day. It tells you how to think, how to dress, how to walk, how to talk, what you should spend your money on, and even how to treat people.... Garbage in, garbage out!" I sat there pondering what the Lord may be getting at, teaching me all of these lessons on love. He was letting me know that love is not a feeling, it's a commitment that is not only contractual, but also a covenant. A covenant is an agreement to your spouse, that no matter what happens the love that is shared is not based on conditions - the ups and downs - of the relationship. A covenant says, "No matter what you do, I'll never withhold my love from you." This is how God loves us and expects us to love our spouse and others.

That night I had a dream that I was in a classroom setting. The assignment was for everyone to write a book, but before we could actually write the book, we had to get a signed consent from specific people. After class was over, I walked around in the hallway outside of the classroom. All of the students seemed to congregate in that area and were talking about the assignment that we needed to complete. There was a shelf of books to my right that caught my attention.

I began to look at them and noticed that all of the books were copies of the same book, it was as if they were being stocked there awaiting shipment. As I looked closer, I noticed that the logo for the company that publishes the books looked like something that was all too familiar to me, it was a white, yet colorful, orb of light that had been printed onto the books.

If I were to compare what it looked like in print form, it looked similar to mother of pearl. As I stood there in amazement, two students talking behind said, "Each book comes with an orb of light." I pondered on this for a second and before I knew it, I felt a presence beside me that I couldn't avoid because of the close proximity. I turned to my left and the teacher was standing there looking at me with a slight smile. I extended my hand out to shake her hand, she looked at my hand for a second and decided that she would shake. As she did, she immediately pulled her hand back. I said, "Oh I understand, you feel what other people feel."

As she looked up at me she smiled again and said, "You have great love for people." After she said that, the dream ended and I was waking up to my alarm.

I started the next day to another one of the Lord's lessons. He began by saying to me, "Don't be held hostage to your compassion for people." I was completely dumbfounded by this statement and had to ask Him what He meant by it. He continued, "You have a strong desire for people to actually experience Me, but not only Me, the best in their lives. If they are willing to take a step, then you are more than willing to help them along the way. You see a little spark in someone and you jump at the opportunity to help them grow. But you can't help everyone. Some people are more content complaining about their current circumstances than actually doing something about them.

These people don't want to grow, nor do they want to see Me. If you try to help people like this on your own accord, they will bring you down and you will become drained for a time."

I was then reminded of Sunday school as a kid. Our teacher told one of us to stand up on a chair and the other to stand on the floor beside the person that was on the chair. He then told us that we as true believers - walking the walk and talking the talk - represent the person that is standing on the chair.

Non-believers and Christians content living in the world represent the person that is standing on the floor. He asked the person on the chair to pull the other person up, no matter how hard the boy on the chair tried, he could not lift him up without the assistance of the person standing on the floor. Then, the teacher asked the boy standing on the floor to pull the person off of the chair. All he had to do was take his arm and just pull slightly and the person on the chair easily fell off.

At that moment, the Lord was reminding me of this lesson to show me how easily a strong believer can be pulled off of their path of growth with Him, if they choose to keep people in their lives that firstly, do not have a relationship with Him. Secondly, if they are Christians but only with the contentment of having the name "Christian" as a nametag and not actually living for Him. Thirdly, Christians who would much rather complain about their life without actually taking a step of faith to watch Him work. Bad company corrupts good morals (1 Cor. 15:33). I began to cry, because in that moment I realized that my ex girlfriend was one of those individuals. He was telling me that it was okay to leave them where they are and keep moving forward with Him. He would take care of the situation in their lives. He is the Savior, not me.

Later in life, He showed me something that I could add to this. He wanted to show me something very important that Jesus did throughout the Bible that is prevalent in a lot of His teachings, and that also related to my situation. He began by using *The Rich Man And The Kingdom Of Heaven* (Matt 19:16-24):

> [16] Just then a man came up to Jesus and asked, "Teacher, what good thing must I do to get eternal life?" [17] "Why do you ask me about what is good?" Jesus replied. "There is only One who is good. If you want to enter life, keep the commandments." [18] "Which ones?" he inquired. Jesus replied, "'You shall not murder, you shall not commit adultery, you shall not steal, you shall not give false testimony, [19] honor your father and mother,' and 'love your neighbor as yourself.'" [20] "All these I have kept," the young man said. "What do I still lack?" [21] Jesus answered, "If you want to be perfect, go, sell your possessions and give to the poor, and you will have treasure in heaven. Then come, follow me." [22] When the young man heard this,

```
he went away sad, because he had
great wealth. 23 Then Jesus said to
his disciples, "Truly I tell you,
it is hard for someone who is rich
to enter the kingdom of heaven. 24
Again I tell you, it is easier for
a camel to go through the eye of a
needle than for someone who is rich
to enter the kingdom of God."
```

After bringing this parable up to me, He said, "Pay close attention to what Jesus did here. The man came up to Jesus to ask Him how to enter the kingdom of heaven and when Jesus told him that he would have to give up his possessions, the man made his own decision to leave. But, did Jesus chase after him to help, knowing that he was making a decision at that moment not to enter the kingdom of heaven? No. He let the man make his own decision and He let him go. Son, you will have to do the same. Allow people to make their own decisions, even though you know where they are leading and the destruction that those decisions will bring. Then, I need for you to continue walking on the path that I have set for you, not looking back to be held hostage to your compassion."

It was nearing the end of my fast. I would pray and promise the Lord a week of fasting at a time. When I hit the third week, coming up on 21 days, He told me that the 21st day would be the last day that I would need to fast. In all honesty, a lot of people think that it is a struggle to fast. But once you have the correct intentions of the fast - meaning you're not doing it to lose weight or anything other than just humbling yourself before the Lord and growing spiritually or casting out demons - then the Lord will honor it and you will be sustained by the Spirit, not growing hungry. By cutting off food as our main source of sustenance, feeding the flesh, and then relying solely on God by praying and reading the Bible, we are now being fed spiritually which sustains us through our fasting.

SATAN'S SCHEME

Within the last year of me writing this book, the Lord began to show me images in my mind as He was teaching other lessons. The images were of my childhood and growing up through my adolescent years of life. Most of it was spent with me always being on pins and needles simply because I was the source of communication for both of my parents. You see, I was born out of wedlock, my parents were not married when they had me and I was what most would call an accident. Though, I jokingly like to think of myself as the most magnificent accident that walks the face of the earth and there are no accidents with the Lord - all of our steps have been ordered and ordained by the Lord (Prov. 20:24).

By being the in between person, I would deliver messages to a parent based on what I was told to tell by the other parent. If something came up and I forgot, then that would be a source of an argument between both of my parents. I didn't like being in between everything. Arguing and yelling seemed to be a common occurrence in my life and between my parents, they honestly just couldn't get along at all.

The Lord continued showing me images of my childhood and I was looking for the point or the lesson that He was trying to teach me. I didn't want to miss it so I continued watching in my mind's eye. As the images were going through my mind, the

Lord spoke to me and said, "Did you ever notice how everything was YOUR fault in all of the arguments that you had with your girlfriend?" I thought about it for a while and told Him that I did notice that. She blamed me for everything, even her own personal growth and the people that she accepted into her life - the people that weren't real friends, and who had the intent of keeping her in her past lifestyle. He continued and said to me, "All of that began in your childhood."

I had no idea what He was talking about. At that moment He began to show me more images and replays of my childhood. In the replays, one of my parents would blame me for specific things that would occur and make statements like, "because of you _____ happened" or "because of dealing with you _____" or "you're acting just like _____"and somewhere along the way, just to appease my parent, I would accept responsibility for things that were completely outside of my control or know how. I would accept responsibility even for their wrong doings.

He continued, "This was and is a scheme of Satan. He was conditioning you as a child to believe that things were your fault when they weren't. Then when you got older and began to step forward passionately pursuing after Me, your ex girlfriend was doing the exact thing that you had grown so accustomed to as a child. She was sent as a distraction. Did you ever notice how there seemed to be a shroud of confusion around the relationship? You guys were having so much fun, but you seemed to be incapable of making strong decisions and too weak to focus on anything but her. I am not a God of confusion, son. When you were pulled away from her, you were able to be used to heal people, deliver people, and speak life into their lives. But as soon as you would come back to her, you felt as if all of that power was drained from you.

You would never be able to do the things that I have called you to do if you would have stayed in a relationship with her.

This is exactly where Satan wanted you to be, shrouded in a mist of confusion and too drained and debilitated to be able to take care of yourself and fully take up the responsibility of My calling for you." I was completely blown away by what the Lord was telling me and so very thankful that He had brought me out of that relationship with her.

Maybe you are experiencing a similar situation where the Lord has called you to do something, but there is a distraction. Maybe you are called to the ministry and the financial sacrifice is the thing that is preventing you from moving forward. Maybe you feel inadequate and constantly view yourself as so much smaller than the big names in ministry. What is distracting you? No matter what it is, the Lord has the solution, seek Him.

The Lord tells us to give no place to the devil (Eph. 4:27 KJV) and anyone who does allows the enemy to have legal right into our lives. With this said, he will try to use your friends, your husbands, wives, kids, and even your parents to try to infiltrate your life and stop you now so that you never move in the power, identity, and authority later in life. Catch him right while he is speaking and always be on guard, not only for yourself, but also for your family and friends. Rebuke him where he stands and trample over him with the authority provided (Luke 10:19).

He taught me that people who don't take responsibility for their actions never grow and when we take responsibility for their actions, it enables them to continue doing the same thing. Having a passive mindset in life and not keeping your feet firmly planted in the Lord leads to a person looking for everyone else to tell them who they are, rather than resting in the identity that the Lord has already given and confirmed for them. Then, when they don't reach the place that they would like to be in life, they become jealous of others that have the success, but didn't people please to obtain it. They knew who they were in Jesus and didn't need anyone to tell them otherwise. I see this a lot on social media, and sadly many people develop their whole lives based on the likes of others. But in reality, they can't have a conversation in real life and don't have real friends.

He also taught me that many people play the victim along with the passive role. Playing the victim and trying to make people think that the source of the problem is always some outside occurrence or some other person takes the heat off of the victim. By taking the heat off of the victim, they truly see themselves as a person that does no wrong - in the case of my ex girlfriend and my parent - which in turn leads to no growth. You can't grow from something that isn't your fault in the first place, especially if you TRULY believe that it's not your fault.

Here are a few promises from the Word concerning who the Lord has told us that we are as believers in Him:

> [5] Even when we were [spiritually] dead and separated from Him because of our sins, He made us [spiritually] alive together with Christ (for by His grace—His undeserved favor and mercy—you have been saved from God's judgment).
> [6] And He raised us up together with Him [when we believed], and seated us with Him in the Heavenly places,

[because we are] in Christ Jesus.
(Eph 2:5-6 AMP).

[17] And if [we are His] children, [then we are His] heirs also: heirs of God and fellow heirs with Christ [sharing His spiritual blessing and inheritance], if indeed we share in His suffering so that we may also share in His glory. (Rom 8:17 AMP)

[9] But you are a chosen race, a royal priesthood, a consecrated nation, a [special] people for God's own possession, so that you may proclaim the excellencies [the wonderful deeds and virtues and perfections] of Him who called you out of darkness into His marvelous light. (1 Pet 2:9 AMP)

[12] But to as many as did receive and welcome Him, He gave the right [the authority, the privilege] to become children of God, that is, to those who believe in (adhere to, trust in, and rely on) His name—
[13] who were born, not of blood

[natural conception], nor of the will of the flesh [physical impulse], nor of the will of man [that of a natural father], but of God [that is, a divine and supernatural birth—they are born of God—spiritually transformed, renewed, sanctified]. (John 1:12-13 AMP)

⁵ He predestined and lovingly planned for us to be adopted to Himself as [His own] children through Jesus Christ, in accordance with the kind intention and good pleasure of His will—
⁶ to the praise of His glorious grace and favor, which He so freely bestowed on us in the Beloved [His Son, Jesus Christ]. (Eph. 1:5-6 AMP)

⁹ For in Him all the fullness of Deity (the Godhead) dwells in bodily form [completely expressing the divine essence of God].
¹⁰ And in Him you have been made complete [achieving spiritual stature through Christ], and He is the head over all rule and authority

[of every angelic and earthly power]. (Col. 2:9-10 AMP)

¹⁷ But the one who is united and joined to the Lord is one spirit with Him. (1 Cor. 6:17 AMP)

⁶ We know that our old self [our human nature without the Holy Spirit] was nailed to the cross with Him, in order that our body of sin might be done away with, so that we would no longer be slaves to sin. ⁷ For the person who has died [with Christ] has been freed from [the power of] sin. (Rom. 6:6-7 AMP)

²⁷ So God created man in His own image, in the image and likeness of God He created him; male and female He created them. (Gen. 1:27 AMP)

⁵ Before I formed you in the womb I knew you [and approved of you as My chosen instrument], and before you were born I consecrated you [to Myself as My own]; I have

```
appointed you as a prophet to the
nations. (Jer. 1:5 AMP)
```

We should stand firm in the Lord's promises and allow Him to be the change through us, accepting responsibility for our falls and getting back up with the lessons learned.

We are not designed to follow a crowd or the trends of the world around us. We are a peculiar people (1 Pet. 2:9)!

> "THE ONE WHO FOLLOWS THE CROWD WILL USUALLY GO NO FURTHER THAN THE CROWD. THOSE WHO WALK ALONE ARE LIKELY TO FIND THEMSELVES IN PLACES NO ONE HAS EVER SEEN BEFORE."
>
> - ALBERT EINSTEIN

CALL TO ACTION

Sometimes it is difficult for us to admit when we are in the wrong. It is also difficult for us to take correction from God, as it doesn't feel good. But both of these are necessary to grow deeper in our relationship to God and to move out of freedom and humility. If you feel yourself falling off in relationship with God, I encourage you to go on a consecration fast and really shut out the world around you to embrace the Lord. You will be pleasantly surprised at what happens and the growth that takes place after.

CHAPTER 8
THE TRIP BACK HOME

THE WORD FILLED FLIGHT

Every year around Christmas time, I take a trip back to Georgia. This particular time, I would make it a priority to go see my grandmother (on my mother's side), as she was in a hospice and was having complications with her heart. Before I walked out of my house in Oklahoma, I said a prayer as I opened the garage door. I asked the Lord to use me to the highest level that He could possibly use me every single day of this trip back home. I asked for Him to give me divine appointments that were ordered and ordained and to bring people around me that needed to hear a message from Him. Then I left my house and drove to the airport.

When I got onto the plane I originally had a window seat, and there was a girl that was sitting in the middle seat of my section, I asked if I could switch with her so that I didn't have the window seat because I personally don't like the curvature of the wall at the window. There was another woman that was supposed to be sitting in the aisle seat which was the seat that I really wanted but she switched with the girl's husband that was already sitting in the middle seat.

So I ended up with the aisle seat, the girl ended up with the middle seat, and her husband ended up with the window seat. At this point, I was now sitting with a married couple and little did I know that these two would be my first divine appointment of the day.

I had been reading *Seeing In The Spirit* by Praying Medic and in that book he talks about how seeing in the spirit isn't only about seeing open visions (Visions seen in both the natural realm and the spiritual realm at the same time. An example would be seeing an angel standing right in front of your bedroom door.), which was something that I was used to in the past. Seeing in the spirit also incorporates seeing with your mind's eye based on the pictures that the Lord places there while he speaks to you. In my mind I already knew this intuitively, but hadn't made that aspect real in my life other than on my long fast. This was an opportunity for me to test everything that I had read in the book, though I had been experiencing it in my personal life for a while.

I began talking with the couple and asked both of them how long they had been married and they said that they had recently gotten married but have known each other for years. The husband then reciprocated the question and asked me how long I had been married, because I like to wear a ring on my wedding finger as a representation of my commitment to the Lord, but I'm still single as a pringle for now. I shared a little bit about my relationship with the Lord and I began to share the testimony about the three things from chapter 2 in this book, which happens to be the testimony I share the most. After sharing this initial testimony, the Lord began to speak to me and put pictures into my mind concerning every word that I needed to speak into this couple's lives.

I began to share another testimony about when I first began to be able to see in the spirit, though I wasn't seeing strong open visions anymore at the time. Then the Lord led me to share how I fell into the legalistic mindset as well as thinking that I had to work to receive specific things from the Lord. The Lord has already opened up the doors for us to be able to do specific things and when we think that we have to work to be able to obtain them, as if they weren't already given to us, then that leaves us back into a slavery mindset and into a mindset of control. We end up crucifying Christ all over again as if what He did on the cross was not good enough. The Lord told me that this would later be the message for the wife but He wanted me to bring this up in the moment first to let her know that she wasn't the only person that was struggling with it.

While I was talking about the angels, I skipped over the part where the Lord delivered me from porn, masturbation, and sex addiction. It was a strong urging in my heart and in my mind to go back to that part of the story, it was the Lord that was sharing with me and telling me that the husband was struggling with porn and masturbation.

I began by telling them that I never know who I'm talking to, so this topic may make them feel a little bit uncomfortable, but I felt an urging in my heart to share it with them. I began to share how I had been addicted to sex, porn, and masturbation and how I couldn't even go a day without giving in to temptation. I told them that I cried out to the Lord, asking Him for help and now I no longer have the desire, the Lord took it from me. The next day He led me to the verse Psalms 34:17. I told the husband to write the verse down because I knew that I was hearing the Lord clearly concerning his struggle with the same addiction. After I got done sharing, the husband told me that he had just gotten done having a conversation with his wife the week before and was telling her about his addiction to porn.

I paused for a second to gather everything that the Lord was saying, as He was telling me that the husband didn't necessarily feel comfortable in his leadership not only to his wife but to everyone around him. The Lord told me to tell him not to worry about his leadership to his wife or the people around him, and to just read the Bible and leave everything to the Lord.

I continued by telling him when you read the Word, it will tell you everything that you need to do to be a great leader and father because He is our Father in heaven. By reading the Word and allowing the Lord to teach you, you will be the earthly representation of our Father in heaven, as you should be. Right after I said this, the husband jumped in surprise. It impacted him in this way because his wife was pregnant, but she wasn't showing. The Lord had intervened and let me know before he had a chance to open his mouth. The husband began to write down the things that the Lord was speaking throughout what I was sharing that was specifically for him.

Then the Lord directed me back to his wife, and one of the first questions that the Lord led me to ask her concerned how her relationship with her father was. She immediately began by telling me that she had forgiven him and tried to make things seem as if they were a lot better than they actually were, but the Lord was telling me otherwise. She said that she struggled as a child because her father spent so much time at work rather than just spending time with her and her siblings. This caused a lot of conflict in their relationship because as she grew up she felt as if she missed out on the time period she actually needed him and the development of the connection between father and daughter. The Lord wanted for me to teach her the model of forgiveness that He had taught me. He taught me that forgiveness is full circle, and we begin by forgiving the other person in our heart. Then we ask the other person to forgive us - as MOST people who have wronged us will never come to us - for any thoughts of bitterness and acts of resentment, providing an opportunity for them to be set free as well. Lastly, we ask the Lord to forgive us both and then move forward.

After giving her this model of forgiveness I got silent for a little while to listen to what the Lord wanted me to do next. He then continued speaking and told me that the joyful personality that she has is nothing more than just a facade and that she was wearing the personality without actually dealing with the root cause after being deeply hurt. He told me to tell her that we do not change from creating an outward personality, we change from the inside out - and the Lord has to help her in this - meaning that we must face the pain and the heartache so that we can grow from it rather than sidestepping the issue and putting on a happy face. After I said this, she immediately began to cry and told me that she had done that all her life and I was the only person that had ever been able to see it. I let her know that I wouldn't have been able to see it if the Lord hadn't revealed it to me, this is all from the Lord, not from me. I continued by telling her that the Lord wants to help her deal with these things and to rid her of the pain that she has felt in her past, but she will have to stop running and begin to face them with His leadership.

As she was dealing with the things that the Lord was bringing up to her, I sat there quietly and continued to listen for anything that the Lord wanted me to say next. The Lord let me know that even at that time period, Satan was working to destroy the baby that she was carrying. I asked if I could pray for her and the baby she was carrying. She said that I could and after I got done, she let me know that there is a history of birth complications in their family and her mother almost died while she was giving birth to her and it was the same case with her grandmother. At this point, I knew that it was a generational curse and Satan wanted to destroy the mother or the baby before it ever gets a chance to live on this earth. He was using me in spiritual warfare (by this point I had learned how to fight) to break that on the plane right then and there.

Before I left the house I had packed a prayer handkerchief, similar to the handkerchief that Paul touched in the Word, which was used for casting out demons and healing the sick (Acts 19:12-13). This handkerchief had been prayed over and could be used for prayer in people's lives and I had every intention of using it accompanied with healing prayers over my grandmother. While sitting there on the plane, the wife began to tell a testimony about how she has a crazy aunt in Mexico, and how the family believes that some type of witchcraft has been put on her.

They believed the witchcraft to be placed on her son as well. He became abusive toward her aunt, and began to beat her. Right then the Lord told me that he had me pack the handkerchief not to pray over my grandmother with, but to give the handkerchief away so that they could send it to Mexico in the mail and all of the demonic activity in her aunt's and cousin's life would then be casted away and they would be delivered. I looked at the wife as I was telling her this, and she looked at me as if I was crazy and I didn't necessarily believe that she would send it to her aunt. But the Lord later revealed to me and showed me an image of her aunt and cousin sitting at the kitchen table, enjoying a meal. The atmosphere of the home was very peaceful and they were very peaceful after the fact. He also led me to give her the spiritual warfare pamphlet that I packed for myself and we parted ways off of the airplane, never to see each other again. I honestly didn't even want to give them the handkerchief or the pamphlet, I wanted to keep it for myself and possibly buy some candy, pray over it and send it to Mexico, and hope for the same effect. I know that sounds selfish but I'm being honest and real here, I wanted to use the handkerchief for my grandmother but I was obedient anyway, and look at what the Lord did!

THE PRAYER WARRIOR CAR RENTAL CENTER

After I had gotten off the airplane, I went directly to the car rental center as I would need a car to drive around Atlanta and visit family.

After I stepped into the Alamo line, there was a woman that was looking at me. She was smiling and I was too, just thinking about the miraculous thing that the Lord had just done with me on the plane. She asked me why I was smiling and I told her that it was because I have Jesus! She instantly wanted to help me and talk with me and since there wasn't much of a line, she pulled me out of the line and we went over to the automated system together. I asked the Lord to show me something about her and give me a word of knowledge about or for her. I immediately saw an image in my mind of her kneeling down on her knees and praying passionately to the Lord in a small room, similar to what the older woman prayed in the movie War Room. I immediately turned to her and I said, "you're a prayer warrior, aren't you?" She responded and told me that she was. I then proceeded and asked her if she cries a lot during prayer - as this is what I saw in the vision - and she told me that she did. Then she began to tell me about how she intercedes for a lot of people and sometimes she gets very passionate in prayer and she begins to cry.

She asked if the Lord had a word for her. I waited for a second and closed my eyes and all I saw was the word "wait". When I opened my eyes I responded to her and told her that I wasn't sure if this actually meant anything to her, but the only word that I saw in my mind was the word "wait". I didn't receive any confirmation from her to know exactly what that meant, but I'm sure that the Lord had a reason for telling her that. We talked a little bit longer, she told me stories about her daughter and then I prayed over her. Then I left and drove to my dad's house in the rental car that I had just gotten.

DREAM OF THE NEW HOUSE

After getting to my dad's house, I was so excited about the things that the Lord was showing me and using me to do that I immediately began to tell my him about everything that just happened on my trip. We talked about the Lord for a couple of hours, watched a few movies together and then I went to sleep. That night I had a great dream.

In the dream I was in my dad's house, the house that he currently lives in. I woke up and I went into the guest bathroom across the hall. I had the door open as I was flossing my teeth. My dad and I were yelling back and forth and having conversation as I was upstairs and he was downstairs. Before I left my room to go into the bathroom I said a prayer over the house and asked the Lord to let the angels of the Lord to manifest their presence and their power openly in my father's house. While standing there flossing my teeth and talking to my dad, I happened to look in the mirror and my washcloth flew off of the rack by itself.

Instinctively, I knew that it had to be an angel as I had just prayed for them to come and enter the house. I went out into the hallway and started walking down the stairs to tell my dad what just happened. As I did, I began to talk to him and pointed upstairs, immediately the whole house transformed and there was no longer an upstairs. We were now in the living room of a new house and we were unboxing the things from the old house in the kitchen area. Some of the things that we had in boxes began to move on their own and began to place themselves exactly where my father wanted them to be. In the dream I couldn't actually see the angels but I knew that the materials weren't moving themselves and so I said a spiritual warfare prayer at that moment in the dream to be sure that it wasn't anything demonic, but everything kept moving and that was the confirmation that this was from God.

When I woke up in the natural, I brushed my teeth and got ready to go to the gym with my dad. On the ride to the gym, I began to tell him about the dream and when I got to the part about the house transforming, the Lord told me that it was my dad's new house. During this time period, my father and his wife had been looking for a house or had the intentions of having one built themselves. I began to describe what the kitchen looked like and told the rest of the story. After I finished telling my dad about the dream, he told me that they were actually having one built and it would be a ranch, a house with no upstairs. He hadn't told anybody about the blueprints or the house that they intended on building but when we got back from the gym, he showed me the blueprints and the blueprints of the kitchen looked exactly as it did in my dream. My dad said that he had been praying over the house and over the blueprints as he was thinking about it being built.

He made the comment that it is probably why the angels were helping in the moving process of the dream. Having this dream made me even more confident in the things that the Lord had already revealed to me and I couldn't wait to find someone else so that I could give them another message from the Lord through His leadership.

STUDY TO SHOW THYSELF APPROVED

My dad and I went to my aunt's house in order to bring by tables for the Christmas gathering that we would have in a few days. As soon as we came into the house I heard the Lord say, "study group". So I asked my aunt while we were setting up the tables, if she had ever been in a study group before. She told me that she had not been in the study group, but they seem like they are a lot of hard work. I proceeded to tell her that the Lord told me to tell her that she would either be in a study group, or leading a study group in the future.

She then smiled and said in a joking manner, "Ohhhh noooo" as if she was a little anxious to do the work that the Lord had for her to do.

The amazing thing is that I spoke with my aunt in October of 2019. I asked her about what was going on in her life and she told me that she was joining a study group at the time. I got so excited because I was used to deliver that message to her. I got the chance to watch the Lord work and it had been almost a year since I was used to deliver that message. Now it was finally coming to fruition. The Lord is amazing!

THE RUNNING MINISTER

One of the days that my dad and I went to the gym I ended up leaving the one week pass that they had given me. The pass allows me to work out at the gym for a week for free. The manager that was there ended up allowing me to just work out because I think he had seen me previously. After working out, my dad went to the locker room and I slowly began to walk toward the front. When I got to the front, I sat down and the same manager was still standing at the front information area where people badge in. I began a conversation with him and said, "I bet you see some interesting things on those cameras while people work out, probably some pretty hilarious things as well." He replied by saying, "Oh yeah, man. Absolutely. Especially the older people that are working out and have no idea about how to actually use any of the equipment."

We both had a laugh about it and then the Lord began to speak to me. The Lord said, "He used to work at another gym before he started working here". So I said to the manager, "You used to work at another gym before you started working here, huh?" He replied and said that he used to work at the YMCA. After I repeated what the Lord said, He spoke again and said, "he's really good with kids." So, once again I repeated what I heard the Lord speak and said, "you're really good with kids, huh?" He then looked at me with a suspicious look that basically said "How do you know this about me?" - and said, "Uhh, yeah I used to work with them at the Y." Then the Lord dropped the bomb on me and said, "He's a youth pastor." I then asked him, "Are you a youth pastor?"

He said, "I go to church, but honestly man, that's just a lot of responsibility. My mom is a theologian and my dad and brother are both pastors. That's just a lot of responsibility and I've seen the behind the scenes of their life, it's a lot." I looked at him for a second, paused and said "Well, the Lord just told me that you're a youth pastor." He replied and said, "Yeah, well that's not the first time that He's told me that I'm a youth pastor." I smiled and said, "Yeah, I tried to run from God, too! I didn't want to accept who He had called me to be, but He's never going to stop calling you. He'll send another to come and tell you the same exact thing that you're hearing from me now. It happened to me. His call and His gifts are irrevocable (Rom 11:29), meaning that once He has given you a gift or has called you to do something, He will never take it back. He will continue calling you until the end of your days because that is what you were created, ordered, ordained, and designed to do."

By this time, my dad was there in the front with me and was waiting for me to get done talking with the manager. As we were leaving, the Lord told me that there would be an opportunity for him to begin walking in the way of ministry soon, so I told him just that. The manager then got on the phone to talk to a customer and my dad and I headed out.

THE SINGER AND THE PROPHETESS

My grandmother, my aunt, my cousin, and her daughter were all at my aunt's house a few days before Christmas and I wanted to go over there to see them and to also take a look at some of the amazing food that they were cooking. When I parked the car on the road, I asked the Lord to give me a word for the people inside. When I came into the house, the very first thing that I did was give everyone a hug and we just hung around and enjoyed ourselves for a little while.

My cousin's baby daughter made a sound and when she made that sound the Lord told me that she was going to be a singer. I then looked at my cousin and told her the very thing that the Lord had told me about her daughter. Right after I told my cousin this, she looked at me and said that she had heard that from someone else a few days prior to me telling her that.

My grandma immediately chimed in with excitement, talking to my cousin, and said, "Well, there you go, that's confirmation from the Lord." The Lord spoke to me again and said that He had put lightning in my grandmother's right hand. I had no idea what that meant, but I figured that it would mean something to her.

By the time that I had gotten a chance to talk with my grandmother about this, everyone else had left to get something to eat. I told my grandmother that the Lord told me that He had put lightning in her right hand. She told me that a prophet had previously told her that there is power in her right hand and that she had had dreams about her using her right hand and miraculous things were happening. At the moment though, she was having problems with her right hand concerning her fingers and problems with her wrist that just seems to stem out of nowhere. So I stood beside her and held her right hand and prayed over it for a little while because the Lord let me know at that moment that the enemy was trying to prevent her from being able to use her right hand in the future.

THE WORRYING WAITRESS

For my last 3 days of my trip back to Georgia, I decided that I would stay with one of my best friends. He and his wife had recently gotten married and they owned a brand new house which was absolutely gorgeous. I wanted to spend some time with them and my brother - my other best friend - also came to spend the night at their house as well. After getting there that night we played a few rounds of pool and corn hole then went to sleep.

The next morning we all went to the gym together and after the gym we went to a breakfast restaurant that my best friend had been ranting and raving about. We sat down and began laughing and joking about some old memories and just having a good time making fun of ourselves. I happened to look over at a waitress and as soon as I looked at her the Lord told me that she has three kids, all of them are boys, and that she is really concerned about one of them. I took that as an opportunity to minister to her and when she passed by the table I called her over. I introduced myself, had a short conversation and then said, "How many kids do you have? You have three kids don't you?" She looked at me and said, "Yes." I responded by saying, "All three of them are boys, right?" She said that they were and looked at me with a look of curiosity. I then proceeded and said, "But you're concerned about one of them, aren't you?" She stood there as tears began to well up in her eyes and said, "Well, one of them passed away a few years ago."

Then the Lord led me to tell her that it is okay to grieve for a while, it is okay to mourn for the people that we have had in our lives. But we cannot stay there in that place, because after a while it becomes a tool for the enemy to use to keep us in that place and if you allow him, you will never experience the joy of the Lord which is our strength (Neh. 8:10). Hearing this word really encouraged her and her whole countenance changed. It was like it was freeing for her to look toward the future and seemed like the word gave her the permission she needed, as if she was intentionally holding herself in that place and felt guilty about moving forward.

This was one of the last times that I went out on this trip to Georgia, and it was also the last word that I had for anyone there. I enjoyed my trip and it excited me for everything that the Lord had up ahead and in store for me and my ministry with Him. Let's go!

JUST PRAY AND WALK

Many of us desire to walk in the things that are previously described in this chapter. We want to see the Lord working in our lives the way that He is described working in the Bible. Well, let me tell you something, it's not just going to happen by you sitting around and not moving toward it in faith. One of the many things that people miss in the Bible is that when people prayed, they not only prayed, but they immediately began to walk in that direction. The prayer is the key to the car, but faith is the car and when you combine both then you will burn rubber faster and harder than you can ever imagine.

If you never take a step of faith in these situations of word of knowledge or prophecy or seeing in the spirit or healing or deliverance or even raising the dead, then the majority of the time it will not happen. The Lord gave us everything that we need in order to do all of this as soon as we got saved, but the very thing that the church is lacking is the boldness to go out and actively start DOING the things that He has already said we are fully capable of doing. I hear Christians say, "Well, if the Lord wanted it to happen for me, then He would just make it happen." To me, that's like saying, "the Lord has given me a mouth to eat with and hands to put the food in my mouth, but I don't have to use my hands in order to use the utensils to get the food to my mouth.

I'm just going to pray about it instead and sit there looking at the food until something happens."

Now, I'm not saying that things don't happen with prayer, because it does. But what I am saying is that we're not stepping out of the faith to see these things happen and using prayer as an excuse not to take a bold step. He gave us all hands for a reason, He gave us all feet for a reason, He gave us a mouth for a reason, He taught us how to speak for a reason. But sadly, we are in a state of mind where we don't use any of the tools that He has given us to move out of the things that He has previously told us to do with the power that we already have.

We just make excuses, going to church and being content with hearing about God but not actually knowing Him and actively carrying out the Word. Simply put, some of us don't even believe that these things are possible anymore but all things are possible to those who believe (Mark 9:23), and our faith is justified by our works (James 2:24). So let's get out there and start laying hands on people and praying for healing. Let's get out there and ask the Lord to deliver messages to you so that you can give them to the people. Let's get out there and start doing the Word and moving out of who He has said we already are. We are supposed to be doing greater things than Jesus (John 14:12), so let's start doing it!

Here are a few examples of people in the Bible who prayed and immediately walked in that direction, watching the Lord work as they took a step.

```
Samson prayed to the Lord and
immediately began pushing the
pillars out of faith that the
Lord would provide the strength
```

> (James 16: 28-30).
>
> The servant that was sent to find Isaac a wife first prayed and moved out of faith by saying what he told the Lord he was going to say to the women (Genesis 24:12-19).

The Lord asks Moses why he is crying out to Him, and instead tells him to raise his staff and part the sea so that the Israelites can go through the sea on dry ground (Ex 14:15-16). The Lord had already given him the power, just like He has given us, but instead Moses was waiting just like most of the church is still waiting today. Let's pick up the fork and put the food in our mouths!

CALL TO ACTION

A lot of us have heard stories of what God has done in people's lives and thought to ourselves that the story seems nice, but the type of lifestyle necessary to have that is dull. I remember thinking that and I couldn't have been the furthest from the truth. You see, when we develop a relationship with God and move out of obedience, our life becomes more fulfilling. Why? Because we were designed to have a relationship with our creator, and once we do, we no longer seek superficial intimacy from other places (sex, porn, excessive drinking, drugs, etc.).

We will be in relationship with the source of all things!

Living the life of obedience is the most important thing of everything in the Bible because it encompasses all (love, humility, patience, joy, kindness, etc.). When we are obedient we have nothing to hide or anything to run from. Out of that obedience, we can stand firm in the promises of the Bible and take a step immediately after prayer and watch the fruition of the kingdom of God unfold. I encourage you, pray AND take bold steps of faith and watch the power of the Lord unfold in, around, and through all of your encounters.

....

CHAPTER 9

"I DON'T WANT YOU WHEN YOU'RE FRESH"

FOOTBALL

I began playing football when I was in the ninth grade. It was a get away from all of the constant tension and fighting and arguing that was going on in my household. I was constantly in a state of anxiety, pain, and anger and I needed an outlet to be able to unleash all of those feelings. Little did I know that I actually just needed to learn to forgive people for taking advantage of me. When I first began playing football, I wasn't a guy that was really well known around the school or the type of individual that just attracted attention everywhere that he went. I was the type of guy that stayed to himself the majority of the time. So, naturally when I played I was shy and I was afraid to embrace the oppurtunity that God had given me to be able to push past my mental limitations. I played center the first year of football, and honestly, football was one of the biggest mental struggles that I ever had in my entire life at the time as it forced me to face my fears. I was too afraid to take off my shirt in the locker room because I was a chubby guy. I was naturally just too afraid of what everyone would think of me, regardless of what I did, so I tried to make myself invisible and not call too much attention to myself. Playing the position of center is the most important position of the entire game of football, so naturally I had a lot of attention on me, attention that I wasn't used to. Little did I know that football would be used to change the entirety of the rest of my life. For me, it provided an outlet to break mental barriers and taught me how to fight when things got hard.

My experience with football coaches is that they aren't the type of individuals that will allow you to make excuses for yourself in your life or on the field. They will tell you the way it is, bluntly, and move on their merry little way regardless of how intense they are to you or how hurtful their comments are.

They are this way because they know that life will not be easy on you and football is a sport that will build your character far beyond what most have experienced in their life, at least in my case. I was afraid of all of the jokes that the coaches would make about me every time that I would make a mistake. I was afraid of the jokes that the players would make about me because it was my first year playing football. Yet, the coaches still saw something in me that I did not see in myself. They saw courage and they saw the fight I had inside.

During practices and games, I never hit anyone with any intention in mind. I wouldn't really attack the opponent in front of me and somewhat let them within the gaps of the offensive line out of fear of the pain. I was afraid that if I hit my opponent, it would hurt worse than the impact that I felt by just letting him have his way. I was a passive player.

After playing my first year of football I made it a point to visualize myself being a great football player so that summer I gave it all I had throughout the conditioning practices, and honestly, I was in a position to begin to start. For the first time in my entire life I had built up a sense of confidence because of my visual standing, the places that I brought myself mentally were being used to carry things out physically. After the conditioning practices we would have a week-long football camp, and during camp I made a commitment to myself that I would give everything that I had, the entirety of my efforts, and I did. No longer was I just sitting there while people would hit me or joke or laugh at me, I began to joke back. I wasn't afraid to take off my shirt in the locker room anymore.

I wasn't afraid of what people would think of me anymore. I just wanted to give my best effort. I just wanted to give everything that I had so that when I went home every night I didn't have any excuse as to why I didn't have the success that I saw in my mind. The last 20 minutes of the last day of football camp, moving into my 10th grade year, we were doing board drills. With this particular drill, there is a player on either side of the board, and the objective is to hit each other as hard as we could, buzz our feet, and then battle it out until the coach blows the whistle.

The first time I did it, I hit the other player so hard that his feet buckled up under him and I landed on top of him. The next time we went up against each other, one of my cleats had gotten stuck in the slippery dirt and as he continued to push with his legs I fell backwards and when he landed on top of me, my ankle dislocated. This was the most amount of physical pain that I have ever felt in my life and in an instant everything that I had built mentally and physically was gone.

I was out for the entire next season of football and then I needed rehabilitation after the fact. Even to this day, I have a metal plate in my ankle. During this time, my mental focus and my drive began to dwindle. I no longer had the intensity of the mind that I had once before, I was broken. I had spent so much time developing a mindset that was unshakable and unstoppable and as soon as the visualization of those things was gone, so was the physical components that came along with the mental.

I realized that I was feeling sorry for myself and decided to pick myself up and came back my 11th grade year to play another season. By the time I came back I had lost so much weight. I lost about 30 pounds and the majority of the football players that I knew my ninth-grade year were so much bigger and stronger than me that I was a little intimidated by what I was seeing. One of the first comments out of their mouth as soon as I entered the locker room was about how small I had gotten and how frail I looked in appearance.

Once spring practice started, I did the best that I could to stand out from the crowd. After some of the practice, we would go back to the locker room and watch the film of that particular practice and the coaches would correct our form based on that specific position. At the time, they looked at me very highly and I was very surprised that they thought of me in such a way. These were new coaches and it was very important for me to impress them so that I could be a starting player, I needed to do my best.

When the season began I was playing left guard on offense and even though I wasn't starting I was highly considered as one of the best 11th grade linemen that we had. Because I was one of the best, they began to put me in every play. I was playing on special teams and anywhere else that they needed me. Because I was becoming so highly considered in all of these specific positions I began to become afraid.

As soon as they would begin to start me in any specific position I was always afraid that I would hurt my ankle again and have to go back to square one. So, I began to self sabotage my own growth.

There would only be spurts of me doing well in specific practices, but as soon as I was considered at the top, then I wouldn't perform as well because I knew that if I was constantly at the top then there was more of a potential for me to get hurt (*my thinking at the time*).

I was afraid that I would have to start all over again, I was afraid that once I got to the top I would break my ankle again, I was afraid of the time that it would take for me to get all the way to the top only to fall all over again. I just didn't want to deal with that. Once I began to sabotage my own growth I was no longer considered as one of the best players. Slowly but surely they began to take me off of special teams, I was no longer the second backup to our best offensive guard, and the coaches began to not even consider me a formidable foe during practices. They turned a blind eye to me and in some cases even secluded me.

With football coaches being so blunt and honest about a football player's character, the coaches began to make jokes about me. There was one coach in particular, which was our defensive line coach, that would go out of his way to make jokes about me. He would hold out his hand and look at me - while the other players were doing drills during practice - and would say loud enough for everyone to hear, "every time I'm on the sideline I'm going to reach out my hand just like this and from now on you're going to be my bubblegum boy. Every time I reach out my hand I want you to go get me a piece of bubblegum because that's all you're good for at this point."

All of the other players would laugh and joke because they knew the true potential that I possessed but, because I was afraid, they used the opportunity to lash out at me with jokes. The same coach called me over during one of our practices and grabbed my face mask and he said to me," What is wrong with you?

You are one of the best linemen that I've ever seen in high school football, but somewhere along the way it seems like you just gave up. Now you're playing like you're soft as Charmin. You have to see the fight within yourself."

I looked at him and told him that I was afraid, not of anyone on the field but just of hurting my ankle again. He said to me, "This time period only comes once in your life, you're going to have to rise up and fight because nobody is going to give you anything and nobody is going to feel sorry for you. Stop holding yourself back." After he said this, he just walked away from me and I never had another serious conversation with that coach again as he ended up getting fired from the position.

All of the football players in high school lift weights. We would have a class containing only football players and during this specific class, we were supposed to be maxing out on bench press. The coaches were making a huge effort to make us a lot stronger than what we were, as we were substantially smaller than the majority of the teams that we were playing against.

When it came time for me to max out, this specific football coach had his clipboard up with his max out sheet on top of it. He looked at me and signaled for me to lift the weight. I had a spotter behind me and I was only lifting 185 lbs. I lifted the weight off of the rack and I tried as hard as I could to push it off of my chest after lowering it, I couldn't get the weight up.

We racked the weight back up and then I tried again. But once again the very same thing happened. After this the coach just looked at me and stared with a blank face and he finally opened up his mouth and said, "You gon' let that weight defeat you, huh?" He then shook his head and walked away as if he was disappointed that I wasn't only letting the team down, but I was letting myself down.

He wasn't going to stand and watch me do so. I got the sense that he was completely disgusted by what he saw me doing. He knew that I had the fight inside of me, I was just too afraid to bring it out because of what might happen. I literally cried after this because I knew that he knew that I wasn't giving it my all - I wasn't giving anything my all. I had let fear completely conquer me.

When it came time for the football banquet my 11th grade year I was one of the only three 11th graders that I had not played enough varsity time in order to get their letter for their Letterman's jacket.

This meant that I had to stand up in front of not only the football players but also their parents as the coach gave an excuse as to why I just received a certificate that said, "Thank you for playing."

I didn't say anything for the entirety of the banquet. I was so angry at myself for not giving it my all that I was almost about to cry as I watched the other 11th graders get their letters and their trophies and plaques and becoming player of the year for that particular season. I knew deep down that I was better than majority of the linemen that were in the grade above me and in my grade, I just needed to get over the hump that was plaguing me. I needed to get over the fear of hurting my ankle again. After the banquet the car ride home was quiet.

The mental place that I was processing was cold and dark and I needed it to nurture my imagination and see myself doing everything right in order to be successful in reality. That night I began to saturate my imagination with me doing every step right from the conditioning, to the weightlifting, to the sprints, to the hitting, to the aggression, and even how the coaches would respond to me when I did all of these things - I wasn't going to leave any stone unturned in the football process. I knew what everything was going to be like, as I had done it so many times.

All that was left to do was to carry out the version of myself that I had envisioned.

Even though I had been envisioning all of these things, I also struggled with my old self and the performance that I had seen all along. Sadly, I held onto it longer than I should have and I continued to beat myself up over it. For a short while, I had convinced myself that it would be okay not to play and I decided that I would not come back to play football during my 12th grade year. I told my dad during one of our conversations that I would be sitting in the stands and watching the game with him, as uncomfortable as that felt to say.

Deep down the only reason that I said that was because I didn't want to put so much effort mentally and physically into something only to have it taken away as soon as things began to look up. In my head, it was better to just not even try. But my dad said something to me that I will never forget, he said, "Are you sure that you're just going to quit?" His question stopped me dead in my tracks because I've never been a quitter at anything. No matter how much people have made fun of me I would always just continue to move forward. I always had hope deep down that people would come around at some point and wasn't concerned if they didn't.

I told him once again that I would be sitting in the stands with him, and all he said to me was "okay". He didn't try to give me any type of motivational speech, he was fine with whatever decision that I chose to make in this situation. But, I could tell deep down - judging by his replies - that I was allowing myself to quit and he was upset that I was quitting on myself. He also knew that it was my personal choice to do so and he wasn't going to take that from me.

Over the next week or so I began to think about the conversation that I had with my dad and I thought to myself, what if I could actually do this again? What if?

Once again I had a breakthrough in my mind. I had clarity in terms of my vision and I wasn't going to allow fear to take hold of me. I no longer cared about my ankle. If it broke while I was playing or while I was conditioning or while I was lifting, it would just have to break. I no longer cared about the thoughts of coaches, if they made fun of me, or if they liked what I was doing. I didn't care. I no longer cared about the thoughts of other people as those thoughts are temporary and based on the way that they view you or if they like the things that you do. In all actuality, their opinions didn't matter very much at all. They only matter when they begin to influence your thought patterns and your actions. I decided that I would try out for spring practice for my 12th grade year, and this time, there would be no holds barred. Anyone who stepped in front of me was now my enemy and I was going to take their head off regardless of their stature and regardless of their reputation. It was time for me to stand up and fight because only cowards run and quit and I'm not a coward.

We only grow when we face our fears and I wasn't going to let this fear prevent me from my own personal growth. When spring practice came along, I remember sitting in the locker room with my equipment on, looking around at all of the players and the new faces of individuals that thought that they had what it took to play football. *I remembered my promise to myself, that I wouldn't care about anything, especially the pain, as pain is sometimes necessary for growth.* It's one thing to just sit and think about the growth, but it's another thing entirely to think about it and then make those things manifest, and here was my chance to do so.

I wasn't going to miss it. As we hit the field I remained relatively quiet, but there was an explosion of controlled anger that I constantly walked around with and I was going to use it as my fuel. Everything that people had said about me and my own debilitating thoughts and actions would no longer hold me back. I was free and I was going to show them how free I was.

We began by doing one-on-one drills, and as lineman, this meant squaring up against someone right in front of you and going head-to-head almost the same way that I broke my ankle, just without a board in the middle, which would then be called a board drill. The very first person I hit, I got off of the line so fast and so hard that I lifted him up off of his feet and slammed him to the ground and immediately there was an uproar from the coaches and from those around me, but I wasn't satisfied. I not only wanted to play the rest of spring practice like this, but I wanted to play the entire season like this. I wanted to be known as a force to be reckoned with.

We did the same drill but the next time, I was up against a fullback that was known for laying people out when he ran the ball. I didn't let his reputation stop me, I was giving it my all. As we both clashed we were at a standstill and he was completely surprised that I came off of the ball with that much force. After the fact, he made it a point to give me my props because he didn't know that I could hit that hard.

Later on that week we had a variation of Oklahoma drills where one person stands about 5 yards away and carries the ball while the other person tries to tackle that person head on. When it came my time to go, the coach handed me the football and I remember my heart racing, remembering my promise to myself. The defensive player that I was up against actually went on to play college football. He was really good at tackling, and the first time I went up against him, he laid me out. When I got up, I had the choice whether to give the football back to the coach and allow the next person to go, and initially, that is what I was going to do.

I gave the football to the coach and began to walk back but then something inside of me wouldn't allow me to continue to the back of the line. I went back up to the coach and I asked if we could run that back again. The same thing happened again, he laid me out once more and I slammed the football on the ground and then I yelled at the coach and I said, "Again!" Intensity began to fill the air and the players and coaches that surrounded could feel it as well and the coach began to embrace this moment. He grabbed my face mask and he asked me, "Who are you?"

I looked around for a second thinking to myself that he already knew who I was, but he was looking for a specific answer as if he was looking to give me a specific identity, one that I had not embraced. I said to him, "Uhhhh, Jeff?" He said to me in response, "You're the Beast. Who are you?" I responded in a not so confident manner, "I am the Beast." He asked me again in a louder tone, as if he wanted it to be known not only to everyone around me, but he wanted me to truly believe it - because if I truly believed it, then I would walk out of that belief - "WHO ARE YOU?" I exclaimed at the top of my voice, "I'M THE BEAST!" I ran full speed into the defensive player that was standing in front of me. He laid me out once again and I got back up AGAIN for more.

Honestly, at this point I think that he was beginning to get tired of me getting back up and fighting. I went back at him one more time and once again he laid me out. The coach had to take the football from me so that someone else would have a chance to do the drill, but by this point everyone was fueled off of my motivation.

It ramped up the entirety of the practice and everyone, regardless of whether they were a lineman or not. Everything took place by my transformation into the acceptance of my new identity. I now accepted who I was and I wasn't going to allow the thoughts of others to take that away from me. I had now become accepted by not necessarily following the crowd, but by bringing to the table my own individuality. It opened up the door for others to be their own individual person as well. Most people just followed the standard, but I was the one defining the standard.

From that point on, I was no longer known as Jeffrey. All of the football players were calling me the Beast, especially the coaches. I loved every bit of it. I began to love the atmosphere, the smell of the grass, and my teammates around me.

I was beginning to truly come into my own by the intensity that I had expressed and the undying will of never giving up and always getting back up when I got knocked down. For the rest of that season I led all of the lineman in our high school and was always seen as a silent leader.

My coach would always stand up at the end of our practices and call out some of the the players that he felt really stood out from the crowd. One of those times, he called me out and he told me to stand up. He always spoke about how he never wanted a player when he was fresh. He said that he always wanted to see the player when he was tired because when a player is tired, they are more susceptible to giving up, they are more susceptible to just go through the motions, they are more susceptible to not give things their all.

When he stood me up he said, "This is a player that I would love for most of you to be like, because he has the heart and the courage to continue fighting when he has nothing left.

It's not about what you do when people are watching you, it's about what you do when you're tired and when nobody is watching you. Will you still give it everything that you have? I never want you when you're fresh."

At the end of the season, we had our football banquet, except this time instead of being one of the only ones that walked away with a certificate I walked away with a trophy and plaque. That meant and still means the world to me because that was the first time that I had fully expressed who I was as a person and I was rewarded for it. I fought back instead of just quivering in my boots and running away from the very things that made me feel uncomfortable or the things that I feared. I had conquered the fear and from that point on I would no longer let fear have a grip on me. When my Letterman's jacket came in, I wore it around school after football season and it had "BEAST" written on the back and reminded me of who I was at all times. I wore my identity with pride and nobody could ever take that from me.

FOOTBALL TESTIMONY PLAY-BY-PLAY

Dear reader, thank you for reading this far. I'm happy that the Lord has allowed me to take you along on the adventure that He has led me through thus far in my life and the many lessons that He has taught me through them. Below, I highlight certain sections of the testimony of my football experience and use it to flesh out what the mindset for running the race looks like.

"Even though I had been envisioning all of these things, I also struggled with my old self and the performance that I had seen all along. Sadly, I held onto it longer than I should have and I continued to beat myself up over it."

This is a very common thing for most of us to do, we sit envisioning a life that is better, a better version of ourselves, and even how we can execute it. Everything seems great, and then we start to doubt the vision, things that we were thinking about seem so far reaching from where we are now, and it seems pointless to think outside of the box. Satan loves to use this tactic against believers right when they are nurturing their imagination and cultivating plans based on what the Lord desires for their future. The Lord speaks to us in our visions and in imagery in our mind's eye to develop these plans. But Satan desires to tear them down before they could ever have the possibility of coming to fruition. This is nothing more than an attack from Satan.

He loves to attack our mind and speaks to us through doubt, because once he is successful in the attack, usually our feet are sure to follow in not carrying out the Lord's plans (Matt. 5:28). Satan will try to remind you of all of the bad things that you have done in your past, all of the people that you have hurt, how you should be ashamed of yourself for what you've done, how people won't believe the new version of yourself that the Lord is molding you into. It is much easier to just sit back and continue in the identity of carrying around all of the baggage that Satan is trying to foist upon you at this time, concerning your past life. But this isn't a time to live in the past, my brothers and sisters, this is a time to put Satan in his place and move forward to the path that the Lord has ordered and ordained for you (Prov. 20:24 AMP)!

The next time Satan comes to you reminding you of all of your past dirt, put him in his place by speaking the statement below:

In the name of Jesus, I rebuke you Satan. I have asked the Lord to forgive me, as well as all of the people involved (do so if you have not). I am a precious child of God and I belong to the Lord (Isaiah 43:1-2). You have no place in my mind and I don't receive anything that you are telling me right now. I'm latching onto the identity that the Lord is showing me and there is nothing you can do about it in the name of Jesus. I command you to leave me now and never return in Jesus' name!"

"Anyone who stepped in front of me was now my enemy and I was going to take their head off regardless of their stature and regardless of their reputation. It was time for me to stand up and fight because only cowards run and quit, I'm not a coward. We only grow when we face our fears and I wasn't going to let this fear prevent me from my own personal growth."

As soon as we have accepted the Lord into our lives and He becomes our Savior, the kingdom of God is within us (Luke 17:21).

All that we have to do is begin to exercise that authority. Sometimes it is not very easy because we are stepping into unknown territory, and we will find that our emotions and rationale will fail us, fear will come upon us, and intimidation will stand before us. This is where we have a choice to back down and do what we've always done - fall in line or in our "rightful place" to fear - or believe who the Lord tells us we are and stand up to it, not caring what things look like, and fighting to the very end. We have to be violent in our pursuit to run this race as intended, taking everything by force (Matt. 11:12). The Lord has not given us a spirit of fear, but one of power, love, and of a sound mind (2 Timothy 1:7).

With this said, if there is something that we do fear (praying in public, making not so popular Biblical decisions, not following the worldly crowd, truly forgiving, etc.), realize that it is coming from the enemy and we have the great opportunity to exercise the courage that the Lord has already given us. The Lord hates a coward (Rev. 21:8) and we are not born of them. We're saints, so let's take up our sword with promises of the Bible and tear down the fear in our lives violently, as if we expect something to happen.

"I remembered my promise to myself, that I wouldn't care about anything, especially the pain, as pain is sometimes necessary for growth."

When we first make the decision to actually live out the Word and run this race, we should come into it with the expectation that people will not like it. We should expect to have to endure pain in any form, because we are being molded and shaped into the likeness of Christ. There will be Christians that won't like it because it doesn't fit their religious rhetoric, there will be old friends that won't like it because you refuse to do all of the worldly stuff you used to, there will be family members that won't like it because they can't control you like they did in the past. Continue moving forward in love to those people and be WILLING to lose some of them as well as WILLING to be humiliated in the mindset of not compromising your stance with the Lord to appease them.

"Everything that people had said about me and my own debilitating thoughts and actions would no longer hold me back. I was free and I was going to show them how free I was."

There is a joy that comes after not compromising and standing strong in your faith and hope in the Lord, Jesus Christ. Once you have made up your mind to move forward and not allow your mind to rest on the things that Satan tries to put in your lap, things begin to open up and you slowly but surely you begin to see yourself the way that the Lord sees you. You begin to see all of His Heavenly glory and the new things that He is doing and putting before you (Isaiah 43:18-19). You will be refreshed and ready to execute the plan and the steps that are necessary to fulfill your purpose and the great commission (Matthew 28:16-20).

"I gave the football to the coach and began to walk back but then something inside of me wouldn't allow me to continue to the back of the line. I went back up to the coach and I asked if we could run that back again. The same thing happened again, he laid me out once more and I slammed the football on the ground and then I yelled at the coach and I said, "Again!" Intensity began to fill the air and the players and

coaches that surrounded could feel it as well and the coach began to embrace this moment. He grabbed my face mask and he asked me, " who are you?"

I looked around for a second thinking to myself that he already knew who I was, but he was looking for a specific answer as if he was looking to give me a specific identity, one that I had not embraced. I said to him, "Uhhhh, Jeff?" He said to me in response, "You're the Beast. Who are you?" I responded in a not so confident manner, "I am the Beast."

He asked me again in a louder tone, as if he wanted it to be known not only to everyone around me, but he wanted me to truly believe it - because if I truly believed it, then I would walk out of that belief - "WHO ARE YOU?" I exclaimed at the top of my voice, "I'M THE BEAST!"

There will be times when we first begin running the race and even after running for a while, that the muscle memory of our past will try to infiltrate our actions again. In those times, we have to be conscious of the fact that we are no longer that individual and to carry out that action the same way does not express our true Christ-like identity.

We are going to have to fight to break out of the old self and to embrace the identity the Lord has for us. Once we begin to take steps of faith and leave old things behind, it motivates other believers to begin to start BOLDY doing the Word, rather than just being hearers of it (James 1:22-25). In addition, speaking our identity outloud (as described in the testimony) affirms who we are in Christ, and puts Satan on notice that we now know who we are in Christ - no longer shying away from the authority that we have in Him.

There are a lot of believers that would like to take those steps, but because it is taboo - especially in America - and we hardly see people be bold in faith, it's scary to step out. That is where you come in, creating the ripple effect!

The Lord sees something in you that you don't necessarily see in yourself. It is the same thing that He saw in Moses, who didn't believe that he was capable (Ex. 3:11). It is the same thing that He saw in Jacob/Israel, who struggled with his identity in the Lord, hence the constant name changes and duality between Jacob and his true identity, Israel (Gen. 33:1/34:7/35:15/35:21/37:1/37:3/43:6/46:1). The thing that the Lord saw in them was a facet of Himself that could only be expressed through them. Each of us has an identity and that identity is moving toward the fullness and stature of Christ in sonship and daughtership. There is no one like you and there will never be. He sanctified you and ordained you for the path up ahead (Jer. 1:5). When you begin to believe the Lord in your identity, you begin to walk out of it, and when you begin to walk out of who you are meant to be, people no longer see you, they see the Lord.

"Honestly, at this point I think that he was beginning to get tired of me getting back up and fighting."

I had bullies as a kid, but nobody really knew about them outside of me. Even though my dad didn't know, he gave me advice that I never forgot. Holding up his fist, he said, "When a bully comes to you, pop him in his mouth the FIRST time he does it." You see, bullies like to prey on people that seem weak, just like our enemy. Satan and his minions roam around seeking out Christians that don't know their authority or who they are in Christ so that he can afflict them, possibly to death.

But, when we hit him in his mouth the first time he comes and continue doing so every time that he approaches us, he's going to get tired of coming. By doing this, you are setting a standard upfront that says that you're willing to fight to the death in prayer for yourself, your family, your friends, and the babes in Christ. If a bully knows that he has to fight every single time he approaches the "victim", it's going to discourage him from doing so, he wants it to be easy.

```
Be strong and of a good courage.
Do not be afraid; do not be
discouraged, for the Lord your
God will be with you wherever you
go (Josh. 1:9).
```

Keep getting back up if you get knocked down in the race and stand your ground EVERY TIME, giving no place to the enemy (Eph. 4:27).

BODYBUILDING COMPETITION ("KEEP GOING")

I started lifting weights for football when I was 14 years old and I lifted on and off through high school and in college. I didn't actually start bodybuilding until about 6 years ago. I didn't previously consider it bodybuilding simply because it requires a specific type of diet which consisted of things that help your body to function at its highest level. I competed in my first competition in 2015 and I ended up getting second to last place. Though I looked relatively good, I was competing against guys that were taking steroids on a consistent basis and had been competing for years previously.

Leading up to the competition I struggled with the diet, even though I lost about 60 lbs. I would lose weight and then gain it back in water weight based on some of the foods that I would eat during my cheat meals.

After my first competition, I made a promise to myself that I would push myself as hard as I possibly could. I saw a lot of weaknesses within my physique and things that I could correct concerning my diet and pushing myself in the gym. I still kept the mindset of "not allowing the weight to defeat me" based on my coach from high school. Three years later, there was another competition that came up and I decided that I would compete in a 2018 show. It was a national qualifier, so therefore people from all around the U.S. were flying in to compete at this show.

This meant that the competition would definitely be tough. Since I'm an all natural bodybuilder, I came into the show knowing that I would probably be smaller than a lot of the guys that I was going to be competing against, but I loved the challenge and I was up for it. I needed to make a specific weight for my height class - one hundred and seventy-five pounds - and I was at one hundred and seventy-seven pounds the week of the show. I was panicking because I would be forced to move to a higher weight class which means that the guys in that weight class would be lean with more muscle than me if I did not make that weight.

I was already doing three sessions of cardio every single day, one at 3 in the morning for an hour, another during my lunch break at work for an hour, and another after I completed my lifting workout. My body was at a complete standstill and I could not drop the water that was necessary for me to get under one hundred and seventy-seven pounds.

I was 4 days away from the show and I thought for sure that my body would drop the water weight necessary for me to compete. When I got on the scale this particular morning, and saw that my weight was still stalled out and it was not moving, I literally stepped off of the scale, took a step back, and almost began to cry. I had worked my body all the way down from where I was only to be forced not to be able to compete because I was two pounds away. I had given it everything that I had and I felt as if I didn't have any more to give.

As I stepped back, a tear was about to begin to roll down my face in anger, anxiety, and defeat, knowing that I had given it everything I had. The Lord immediately stepped in and spoke powerfully and said clear as day, "Keep going!" Right after He said this, the tear that was about to roll out of my eye went back into my tear duct and I had this overwhelming sense of peace that came over me.

I went to my bedroom and sat on my bed for about 10 minutes and began to think to myself about how involved the Lord had been in this entire process. Even though during this entire time of preparing for this competition - 6 months - I felt like I had placed the competition at a higher priority than the time that I was spending with the Lord. He still cared and He still wanted me to keep going even though I had put something ahead of Him. I was completely in awe of this and wanted to know why He would do something like that, knowing that I hadn't really been spending the passionate time alone with Him that I normally did.

I asked him why he would do such a thing and permit me to continue going and He told me once again that I should keep going. That same day, one of my workplace friends came up to me at work to ask me about the competition and my preparation for it. He would also be competing in the same class as me and we would be on the stage competing against each other.

I told him that I could not get the last two pounds off and I only had 3 days before the competition. All he did was smile and he invited me to his gym to get the water weight off. For the next 2 days, we went to the gym and would go to the sauna and then immediately walk on the treadmill to get the water weight off. When it came time for the weigh-ins of the competition, I was at 172.5 pounds.

As I walked onto the stage with the other competitors, I asked the Lord to give me favor. I ended up coming in second place and beating out everyone in my class except for one person. This was really special to me because some of the people that I beat were taking steroids. The Lord gave me favor in this competition and I was so grateful for everything that He did in terms of not allowing me to stop when it felt like there was no hope, when it felt like I had done everything humanly possible, and when it felt like I wanted to give up because I had nothing left to give.

As I took a shower in the hotel room the next morning after the competition, I asked the Lord, "Why did You tell me to keep going even though You knew that I had placed the competition at a higher priority than my time with You?" He responded to me and told me, "Because this is how I would like for you to come after me for the rest of your life. You have given this competition everything you had and I want you to draw near to me with everything that you have." I kept this in the back of my mind as I took a shower and I never forgot it. The Lord is always there willing, waiting, and watching us at all times, waiting for us to involve Him in our lives.

KEEP PUSHING
THROUGH THE STRUGGLES

Running this race will not be without any struggles or even sufferings, but this is the very place that we find the Lord and the true depths of perseverance through the Holy Spirit who has been given to us.

> ...but we also glory in our sufferings, because we know that suffering produces perseverance, character, and hope. And hope does not put us to shame, because God's love has been poured out into our hearts through the Holy Spirit, who has been given to us. (Rom 5:3-5)

As Christians we need to go ahead and have it in our minds that this world will not like us because we represent our Father, Jesus Christ. This world hated Him and in turn we will be hated (Matt. 24:9). Because of this and because of what we stand for and who we represent, we will be excluded from certain groups, certain religious church gatherings, certain people won't want to be around us, and some of our life will even require us to walk alone. We may be made fun of, laughed at because of our faith, ridiculed for actually doing the Word versus just going to church, hearing about the Word, reading the Word for ourselves, and doing nothing with it.

[18] "If the world hates you, keep in mind that it hated me first. [19] If you belonged to the world, it would love you as its own. As it is, you do not belong to the world, but I have chosen you out of the world. That is why the world hates you.
[20] Remember what I told you: 'A servant is not greater than his master.'[a] If they persecuted me, they will persecute you also. If they obeyed my teaching, they will obey yours also. [21] They will treat you this way because of my name, for they do not know the one who sent me. [22] If I had not come and spoken to them, they would not be guilty of sin; but now they have no excuse for their sin. [23] Whoever hates me hates my Father as well. [24] If I had not done among them the works no one else did, they would not be guilty of sin. As it is, they have seen, and yet they have hated both me and my Father. [25] But this is to fulfill what is written in their Law: 'They hated me without reason.
(John 15:18-24)

It is time for us to rise up and be bold in our faith and preaching the Word to all creation (Mark 16:15), not caring about what other people think of us. Let's step out of the common mindset of just going to church and watching football on Sundays, thinking that this is a true Christian walk. Let's get up and actually start fighting for the things that we believe in and when I say fighting, I mean actually going out and actively doing the Word.

This could come in the form of going to Walmart just to minister to people about the Word, or ministering to people in your workplace, or sharing specific testimonies of breakthrough of the Lord when someone is struggling with specific things that the Lord has already brought you out of. Our testimonies carry so much power and so much weight and people are much more inclined to listen to your personal testimony of the Lord than to have you Preach at them about what they personally need to be doing. Too many of us have forgotten that this journey isn't about the full expression of ourselves, but it is about the full expression of the Lord through us and how human we are without Him.

We as Christians have become concerned with what other people would think of us if they knew the dirt in our lives, but everyone has a beginning and it is wrong of us to think that by sharing the dirt that the Lord brought us out of, that He can't use that testimony to set others free (Rev. 12:10-11).

This is why it is so very important for us to not only preach the Word but to share our testimonies moving out of vulnerability, which can sometimes be a level of perseverance through the fear of the thoughts of others. We have to keep going in pursuit of not only the Word and the Lord but also doing the Word and allowing ourselves to be vulnerable and weak - through the sharing of our past - so that we may be used in full expression of the Lord (2

Cor. 12:9). The Word tells us that the testimony of Jesus is the spirit of prophecy (Rev. 19:10). In addition, it tells us that we overcame the enemy by the blood of the Lamb and the Word of our testimony (Rev 12:11).

This means that our testimonies carry power and that power can be used in the same way that it was used in your life as a prophecy to another person's life to set them free. But if we just remain quiet and sit there, being insensitive to the power that we contain, we may never see the power of God released as a body of Christ. So, let's actively and intentionally get out of our comfort zone and start running this race! It won't be without struggle, but let's persevere and keep going to express the only Hope this world has, Jesus Christ.

NOT SO LINEAR

Running the race and living as a Christian is not a lifestyle that will be without its ups and downs. We will struggle and we will always fall short of the glory of God because none of us are perfect. But thankfully, the Lord isn't looking for anyone that is perfect, He is looking for people who are willing. He is looking for the people who are willing to stay strong in their faith and not compromise, He is looking for people who will take bold steps of faith regardless of what people will think of them, He is looking for us to continue fighting and being obedient even when it seems like there is no way out and no light in the darkest of times. Paul gives us instructions about running the race and what the race looks like in 2 Timothy 4:1-8:

In the presence of God and of Christ Jesus, who will judge the living and the dead, and in view of his appearing and his kingdom, I give you this charge: ² Preach the Word; be prepared in season and out of season; correct, rebuke and encourage—with great patience and careful instruction. ³ For the time will come when people will not put up with sound doctrine. Instead, to suit their own desires, they will gather around them a great number of teachers to say what their itching ears want to hear. ⁴ They will turn their ears away from the truth and turn aside to myths. ⁵ But you, keep your head in all situations, endure hardship, do the work of an evangelist, discharge all the duties of your ministry. ⁶ For I am already being poured out like a drink offering, and the time for my departure is near. ⁷ I have fought the good fight, I have finished the race, I have kept the faith. 8 Now there is in store for me the crown of righteousness, which the Lord,

> the righteous Judge, will award to
> me on that day—and not only to me,
> but also to all who have longed
> for his appearing.

From the moment that we set foot on this Earth, one thing is guaranteed, and that one thing is that we will all die one day. Begin to use this as your motivation until passion begins to fuel you because motivation is nothing more than just a spark. Develop the heart of courage that is necessary to stand up when it seems like everyone around you, even other Christians are compromising and living for the world. Move out of your faith and allow the Lord to use you to do the miraculous out of your personal relationship with Him. Hold captive your carnal imaginations and put them into the submission of the Lord (2 Cor. 10:5).

Visualize yourself healing the sick, raising the dead, casting out demons, conquering fear, and standing bold in your faith and not compromising. Nurturing your thoughts and imaginations daily on the things above and the great commission makes the reality of those things definite. Turn your foot sideways and kick your foot down Satan's throat and every scorpion and serpent that comes your way, as the Lord gave us feet for a reason (Luke 10:19). This world won't like you and will never accept you and you have to be okay with that. Just as my coach said, "I don't want you when you're fresh." What are you going to do when times get hard? What are you going to do when no one is watching? RUN THIS RACE!

CALL TO ACTION

Many of us have found ourselves in positions that seem as if there is no way out. The struggle seems as if it is too big for us to handle and like there is nothing that we can do to stand firm and fight as we are completely exhausted. It is in these very moments that we realize the Lord has allowed for these situations to happen to build our character for the fight up ahead and the path that He has ordered and ordained all of us to walk. When you are ready for the fight ahead of you in your life, say the below prayer and watch it manifest in your life.

"Lord, help me to be a walking, talking representation of you no matter how hard the journey gets. Let me not only be an ambassador for You through words, but also in demonstration. Help me to walk and run the race in a way that is uncompromising and is ferocious and terrifying to all forms of the enemy and his trappings. Help me to be a demonstration of Your holy light to those around me, shattering doubt everywhere I go. Amen."

CHAPTER 10
MESSAGE TO THE READER

PRAYER TO RUN THE RACE

If you are a Christian and have never experienced the Lord in the ways described in this book and would like to experience similar adventures, then the below prayer is for you! Get out there and take steps of faith and let's run this race together!

"Father In Heaven, I ask that you open me up to better experiences than the ones described in this book and help me to move out in the faith necessary to make all of it happen. Help me to remain steadfast and not falter to the left or to the right when it comes to compromising any of the Word and my personal relationship with you. Help me to take bold steps of faith into darkness and be a beacon of your righteousness and light everywhere that I go, shattering the forces of darkness that stand before me and those around me. I ask that you make me invisible to the enemy and teach me how to use the weapons of Salvation, Righteousness, Truth, Peace, Faith, and the Word. Help me to persist in speaking God's Word until it accomplishes its purpose.

PRAYER OF SALVATION

If you have stumbled upon this book and would like to receive the greatest gift of all, salvation, and allow the Lord Of All, Jesus Christ, to come into you and your life please read the below prayer aloud. When you pray it, really mean it, don't just say the words but also believe them in your heart (Rom. 10:9). He's waiting for you!

"Lord Jesus, I acknowledge that I am a sinner and that sinning has been a way of life for me. I ask that You forgive me of my sins and wash me clean. I receive you as my Lord and Savior into my life and I ask that you order and ordain every step of the path ahead of me.

Sanctify my walk, talk, and state of mind from this point on and guide me into the perfection of my personal ministry. Anoint me with the oils of joy (Heb. 1:9) and set me ablaze with undying passion for you. I ask that you begin my journey right after saying this prayer and break every strategy of darkness that is assigned to prevent me from taking steps of faith. Help me to be confident in you and the journey we have ahead. Open me up to experiences like the ones provided in this book and help me to recognize when it is You. Please close every door that doesn't need to be open and leave the doors open that you want me to go through. Please take everyone out of my life that does not need to be there and bring people into my life through divine appointment, that will help me get to where You'd like to lead me. Equip me Lord, and prepare me for the fight up ahead. I'm ready to run the race! Amen."

Thank you for reading, I recommend that you get a Bible reading plan and just read the designated passages as you begin your adventure with the Lord. Your journey awaits, get out there and let's run this race together!

DECREES

The Lord tells us that when we decree a thing, it will be established unto us (Job 22:28). Below are two of my personal decrees, feel free to say them for yourself or use them as structure to create your own based on the Lord's leading. They have shaped my life, since 2017, after I started reading them outloud before I start my day in the mornings. I can honestly say that they are coming true at the time of me writing this book. I hope they are a blessing to you and aid in your adventure alongside the Lord.

Decree 1: "I decree that I am a Godly warrior fighting alongside angels that He has given charge over me to win souls. I persist in speaking God's word until it accomplishes its purpose. It is like a fire. It is like a hammer that shatters a rock (Jer. 23:29). I am strong and courageous in my pursuit to bring overwhelming light everywhere that I am. I am not afraid, neither will I be dismayed for the Lord is with me wherever I go (Josh. 1:9). I decree on the authority of the Word that my spiritual senses are open and clear at all times in the pursuit of total obedience, humility, and honor to God. I will lead those without the slightest bit of hope as I am being strengthened by the power according to His might. I have great endurance and patience through Christ (Col. 1:11). I decree that no weapon formed against me, natural or supernatural, shall prosper (Isa. 54:17) as Christ breaks barriers, casts out demons, gives hope, and dismisses doubt through me. I will be used as an overpowering beacon of light to accomplish His will as God has not given me a spirit of fear, but has given me a spirit of power, love, and of a sound mind (2 Tim. 1:7)! Amen!"

Decree 2: "I decree that I am a powerful new creation in Christ. My individual essence has completely changed and I am a being in Christ as He is in me. I will not water down the Gospel to accommodate people, nor will I give into the flesh at the sacrifice of the spirit. I will follow, seek, and live in the spirit of Christ NO MATTER WHAT, constantly feeding the spirit. I will be used as a Godly warrior in the spirit and in the natural, fighting demons alongside angels, delivering blessings to different regions, going on Godly missions for God, seeing in the spirit, taking visits to heaven, having conversations with Jesus face-to-face, having a personal relationship with the angels, creatures, and heavenly hosts that are assigned to me (all of this in the spirit). In the natural, I am used to prophesy, heal the sick, raise the dead, speak in tongues, change the atmosphere, encourage, see in the spirit, deliver miracles, interpret dreams, and discern the spirits. I decide with my whole heart to enter through the door of the cross, humiliating myself, obeying God, and renouncing the pleasures and the rudiments of the world. I AM ONLY SATISFIED WHEN GOD IS PLEASED."

BOOKS I RECOMMEND

BIBLE READING PLAN

- *One-Year Bible Reading Plan* - Rose Publishing

SPIRITUAL WARFARE

- *Destroying Fear* - John Ramirez
- *Armed And Dangerous* - John Ramirez
- *Spiritual Warfare Prayers (pamphlet)* - Mark I. Bubeck
- *Shaking The Heavens* - Ana Mendez
- *Demon Hit List* - John Eckhardt
- *The Full Armor Of God* - Larry Richards
- *Protecting Your Home From Spiritual Darkness* - Chuck D. Pierce
- *Fasting For Breakthrough And Deliverance* - John Eckhadt
- *End Time Warriors* - John Kelly

SPIRITUAL SIGHT & TRAVEL

- ALL books written by Michael Van Vlymen
- ALL books written by Bruce Allen (Especially *Gazing Into Glory*)
- *Traveling In The Spirit Made Simple* - Praying Medic
- *Seeing In The Spirit Made Simple* - Praying Medic

LOVE & RELATIONSHIPS

- *A Loving Life* - Paul E. Miller
- *Love Walked Among Us* - Paul E. Miller
- *Every Man's Battle* - Stephen Arterburn & Fred Stoeker
- *Every Young Man's Battle* - Stephen Arterburn & Fred Stoeker
- *The Sacred Search* - Gary Thomas

APOLOGETICS

- *Standing For Truth* - Crossings Ministries
- *I'm Glad You Asked* - Ken Boa & Larry Moody

ABOUT THE AUTHOR

Jeff Thomas is an online minister, author, and Godly motivational speaker/preacher with a heart to strengthen the body of Christ and lead them into a deeper relationship and experience with God.

CONTACT INFORMATION

To book Jeff to speak to your congregation, gathering, or event, call or email:

Phone: 918-766-9673
Email: winsouls888@gmail.com

To watch his motivational videos, visit:
www.youtube.com/winsoulstv

OTHER MEDIA:

Website: Winsouls.net | Facebook: jeffrey.r.thomas.14
Instagram: win_souls8 | Twitter: @JeffreyThomas13

REFERENCES

Medic, P. (2015). *Seeing in the spirit made simple.* Gilbert, AZ: Inkity Press.

Miller, P. E. (2014). *A loving life: In a world of broken relationships.* Inter-Varsity Press.

Pierce, C. D., & Sytsema, R. W. (2014). *Protecting your home from spiritual darkness.* Grand Rapids, MI: Chosen Books.

R., V. V. (2016). *Supernatural transportation: Moving through space, time and dimension for the kingdom of heaven.* Place of publication not identified: Ministry Resources.

Vlymen, M. V. (2013). *How to see in the spirit.* Carmel, IN: River of Blessings International Ministries.

www.ingramcontent.com/pod-product-compliance
Lightning Source LLC
Chambersburg PA
CBHW030907080526
44589CB00010B/182